THE

POCKET
IDIOT'S
GUIDE™ TO

Spanish Phrases

Third Edition

by Gail Stein

A

ALPHA

A member of Penguin Group (USA) Inc.

ALPHA BOOKS

Published by the Penguin Group

Penguin Group (USA) Inc., 375 Hudson Street, New York, New York 10014, USA

Penguin Group (Canada), 90 Eglinton Avenue East, Suite 700, Toronto, Ontario M4P 2Y3, Canada (a division of Pearson Penguin Canada Inc.)

Penguin Books Ltd., 80 Strand, London WC2R 0RL, England

Penguin Ireland, 25 St. Stephen's Green, Dublin 2, Ireland (a division of Penguin Books Ltd.)

Penguin Group (Australia), 250 Camberwell Road, Camberwell, Victoria 3124, Australia (a division of Pearson Australia Group Pty. Ltd.)

Penguin Books India Pvt. Ltd., 11 Community Centre, Panchsheel Park, New Delhi—110 017, India

Penguin Group (NZ), 67 Apollo Drive, Rosedale, North Shore, Auckland 1311, New Zealand (a division of Pearson New Zealand Ltd.)

Penguin Books (South Africa) (Pty.) Ltd., 24 Sturdee Avenue, Rosebank, Johannesburg 2196, South Africa

Penguin Books Ltd., Registered Offices: 80 Strand, London WC2R 0RL, England

International Standard Book Number: 978-1-59257-453-7
Library of Congress Catalog Card Number: 2005933826

08   8 7 6

Interpretation of the printing code: The rightmost number of the first series of numbers is the year of the book's printing; the rightmost number of the second series of numbers is the number of the book's printing. For example, a printing code of 05-1 shows that the first printing occurred in 2005.

Printed in the United States of America

Note: This publication contains the opinions and ideas of its author. It is intended to provide helpful and informative material on the subject matter covered. It is sold with the understanding that the author and publisher are not engaged in rendering professional services in the book. If the reader requires personal assistance or advice, a competent professional should be consulted.

The author and publisher specifically disclaim any responsibility for any liability, loss, or risk, personal or otherwise, which is incurred as a consequence, directly or indirectly, of the use and application of any of the contents of this book.

Most Alpha books are available at special quantity discounts for bulk purchases for sales promotions, premiums, fund-raising, or educational use. Special books, or book excerpts, can also be created to fit specific needs.

For details, write: Special Markets, Alpha Books, 375 Hudson Street, New York, NY 10014.

This book is dedicated to my patient proofreader husband, Douglas; my skilled, computer-consultant son, Eric; my most ardent fan and son, Michael, and his terrific wife, Katherine; and my parents, Sara and Jack Bernstein, whose love and support have helped me become the woman I am today.

Contents

Introduction

So you want to speak Spanish. Is it because a sexy, Latino accent makes your heart skip a beat and your legs start to wobble? Perhaps it's because the aroma of fine, home-cooked paella makes your stomach growl in eager anticipation of an extraordinary repast. Or is it because seductive ads containing the beautiful white sands and blue waters of Cancun's beaches beckon you at vacation time? Whatever your reasons for wanting to learn the language, this book will help you achieve quick and easy results.

Take a long, hard look around you—Spanish is everywhere. There's no time like the present to familiarize yourself with words, phrases, and expressions that can come in handy on a daily basis. In no time flat, you'll appreciate the advantages that a knowledge of Spanish can bring you, no matter what the situation.

What's on the Inside

You will learn pronunciation and grammar painlessly and effortlessly without sacrificing speed and accuracy. Whether you're a student, a traveler, or a business person, this book will teach you the basics while giving you the vocabulary and the phrases you'll find most useful in almost every conceivable daily situation. You'll be introduced to a wide variety of topics: food, clothing, sports, health, and much more.

This book is not merely a phrase book, a grammar text, or a travel guide—it's a combination of all three. That makes it not only very unique but an extremely useful tool for people who want a working command of the Spanish language. It will allow you to understand and to be understood without embarrassment or frustration and with ease and enjoyment. Yes, learning Spanish can be fun!

This book was written with you in mind. That's why it's so user-friendly. By the time you've read it through, you'll be a pro at ordering a meal to suit your diet, watching a Spanish film without depending on the subtitles, finding the perfect meringue partner, dealing with security personnel before they perform a full body search at the airport, getting the biggest bang for your bucks, and replacing the contact lens you lost while scuba diving. You'll be amazed and surprised at how rapidly you'll learn what you need to know.

In addition to all the vocabulary lists, phrases, grammatical explanations, references, and pronunciation guides, this book contains lots of extras presented in sidebars throughout the text:

Something Extra

Look here for extra tips and hints about the language.

¡Cuidado!

Watch out! These boxes indicate pitfalls and traps you want to sidestep.

Acknowledgments

Thank you! Thank you! Thank you to some very special people who have made a difference in my life and have greatly enriched it. A special "I love you!" accompanied by hugs and kisses to the following:

Ray Elias for ensuring that the local bookstores keep Stein in stock and for being an even greater guy 40 years later.

Roger H. Herz for being a fabulous consultant.

Marty Hyman for giving me the best legal advice imaginable.

Christina Levy for being the best advisor and confidante in the world.

Terry Bordan for giving me constant encouragement.

And thanks to the people at Alpha Books.

Special Thanks to the Technical Reviewer

The Pocket Idiot's Guide to Spanish Phrases, Third Edition, was reviewed by an expert who double-checked the accuracy of what you'll learn here, to help us ensure that this book gives you everything you need to know about Spanish phrases. Special thanks are extended to Clark Zlotchew.

Trademarks

All terms mentioned in this book that are known to be or are suspected of being trademarks or service marks have been appropriately capitalized. Alpha Books and Penguin Group (USA) Inc. cannot attest to the accuracy of this information. Use of a term in this book should not be regarded as affecting the validity of any trademark or service mark.

The Gringo's Quick Pronunciation Guide

Even though Spanish is a foreign language, it's very easy to pronounce because it is very phonetic. It's that simple! Just say each word exactly as you see it and add a Spanish accent. Chances are, you'll sound remarkably like a native speaker—well, close to one anyway.

Accentuate the Positive

You will notice that there are three accent marks (more properly called diacritical marks) in Spanish:

- The ´ simply indicates that you put more stress on the vowel.
- The ˜ only appears over an *n*. It produces the sound "ny" as in the first *n* in union. The *ñ* is considered a separate letter.
- The ¨ is used when there is a diphthong (two vowels together). It indicates that each vowel must be pronounced separately.

¡Cuidado!

All letters in Spanish are pronounced except the letter *h*, which is always silent. The letter *v* is pronounced like the English *b*. The *k* and the *w* are used only in words of foreign origin.

Different Strokes for Different Folks

The following pronunciations are for the Spanish spoken in South and Central America and in certain areas of southern Spain.

Letter	Sound	Example	Pronunciation
		Vowels	
a	ah	Ana	ah-nah
e	eh	entrar	ehn-trahr
i	ee	idea	ee-deh-yah
o	oh	oficina	oh-fee-see-nah
u	oo	usar	oo-sahr
		Diphthongs (Vowel Combinations)	
ae	ah-yeh	aeropuerto	ah-yeh-roh-pwehr-toh
ai	ah-yee	aire	ah-yee-reh
au	ow	auto	ow-toh
ay	ahy	hay	ahy
ea	eh-yah	reacción	rreh-yahk-see-yohn
ei	eh-yee	beisból	beh-yees-bohl
eo	eh-yoh	feo	feh-yoh

Letter	Sound	Example	Pronunciation
eu	eh-yoo	Europa	eh-yoo-roh-pahey
	eh-yee	rey	rreh-yee
ia	ee-yah	Gloria	gloh-ree-yah
ie	ee-yeh	fiesta	fee-yehs-tah
io	ee-yoh	avión	ah-bee-yohn
iu	ee-yoo	ciudad	see-yoo-dahd
oa	oh-wah	toalla	toh-wah-yah
oe	oh-weh	oeste	oh-wehs-teh
oi	oy	oiga	oy-gah
oy	oy	soy	soy
ua	wah	guardar	gwahr-dahr
ue	weh	cuesta	kwehs-tah
ui	wee	cuidado	kwee-dah-doh
uo	oo-oh	continuo	kohn-tee-noo-oh
uy	wee	muy	mwee
		Consonants	
b	b	bueno	bweh-noh
c	soft c (s) before e, i	centro	sehn-troh
	hard c (k) elsewhere	casa	kah-sah
ch	ch	Chile	chee-leh
d	d	dos	dohs
f	f	favor	fah-bohr
g	soft g before e, i	general	heh-neh-rahl
	hard g elsewhere	gracias	grah-see-yahs

continues

continued

Letter	Sound	Example	Pronunciation
h	silent	hombre	ohm-breh
k	k	kilo	kee-loh
l	l	lista	lees-tah
ll	y	llama	yah-mah
m	m	madre	mah-dreh
n	n	nada	nah-dah
ñ	ny	año	ah-nyoh
p	p	padre	pah-dreh
q	k	Quito	kee-toh
r	r (small roll)	salero	sah-leh-roh
rr	r (large roll)	carro	kah-rroh
s	s	sí	see
t	t	toro	toh-roh
v	b (less explosive English b)	vender	behn-dehr
x	s, ks	extra	ehs-trah
		exacto	ehk-sahk-toh
z	s	zoo	so

All About Stress

The rules for stress in Spanish are rather straight-forward but do require some study:

- If a word ends in a vowel, an *n*, or an *s*, place the stress on the next to the last syllable, for example: *camisa, imposible, muchacho, examen, tipos.*

- If the word ends with any other letter besides those mentioned above, the stress is on the last syllable, for example: *pastel, hablar, juventud.*

- All exceptions to the above two rules have an accent over the vowel of the stressed syllable, for example: algún, lámpara, inglés, médico.

The only exceptions to these rules are for words of foreign origin, usually words taken from English, which retain their original spelling and pronunciation, for example: sandwich, e-mail.

Unlike English, where words are often phonetically confusing, difficult to sound out, and contain syllables with varying amounts of stress, Spanish words are pronounced exactly as they are written.

Something Extra

The Spanish *r* is always rolled. Give it something extra when the *r* comes at the beginning of the word. The *rr* is always rolled a lot (about three trills).

A Course of Action

In This Chapter

- Getting off to a good start
- What you already know
- Idiomatic Spanish

So you want to learn Spanish, and you want to learn it fast. The easiest and most efficient way to accomplish this goal is just to plunge right in. Totally immerse yourself in anything and everything Spanish. The trick is to have a love affair not only with the language, but with the culture as well.

Let Us Begin

Follow these suggestions if you want to quickly develop a long-lasting, fulfilling relationship with Spanish:

- Be honest with yourself. What exactly are your goals? How much linguistic ability do you possess? Do you have a good ear for language? Determine how much time each day you want to devote to Spanish and stick with it. Proceed at your own pace. There's no rush!

- One way or another, get your hands on a good bilingual dictionary. Pocket varieties (which usually cost between $6 and $15) might suit the needs of some learners, but can prove somewhat deficient for others. The following are among the more popular, easy-to-use, and comprehensive dictionaries, with a wide range of up-to-date, colloquial, and idiomatic words and phrases:

     HarperCollins (approximately $55)

     Larousse (approximately $60)

- Listen to Spanish whenever you can. Never miss an opportunity to become involved with the language. A wide selection of foreign films is available at large video stores. Public radio and television broadcast many Spanish programs. Look and listen! Borrow language tapes from your local library and pay attention to the sounds of Spanish.

- Read everything you can get your hands on. Read to yourself or out loud to your mirror. Practice your comprehension and your pronunciation all at once. Pick up a Spanish newspaper (*El Diario* or *La Prensa*, for example) and focus on what's happening in the Hispanic world.

- Find the perfect spot in your home to serve as *un rincón español* (a Spanish corner). Dedicate this area to your new project. Make it look the part.

Something Extra

Your knowledge of Spanish is undoubtedly more extensive than you realize. That's right. You know more than you think. Chocolate, potatoes, tomatoes, taxi, patio, piano, alpaca, mosquito—the list of Spanish words used in English is surprisingly long!

The Cognate Connection

Want to pick up Spanish really quickly? Learn your cognates! What are they? Quite simply, a *cognate* is a word spelled the same (or almost the same) as a word in English and that has the same meaning. Sometimes we've actually borrowed a word from Spanish, letter for letter, and have incorporated it into our own vocabulary. Sure, cognates are pronounced differently in each language, but the meaning of the Spanish word is quite obvious to anyone who speaks English.

Want to get a jump-start on your list? Tables 1.1 and 1.2 provide lists of words that are the same (or almost the same) in both languages.

Table 1.1   Exact Cognates

Adjectives	Masculine Nouns El (ehl)	Feminine Nouns La (lah)
cruel (kroo-ehl)	actor (ahk-tohr)	banana (bah-nah-nah)
grave (grah-beh)	animal (ah-nee-mahl)	fiesta (fee-yehs-tah)
horrible (oh-rree-bleh)	color (koh-lohr)	hotel (oh-tehl)
natural (nah-too-rahl)	hospital (ohs-pee-tahl)	radio (rrah-dee-yoh)
tropical (troh-pee-kahl)	motor (moh-tohr)	soda (soh-dah)

Table 1.2   Almost Exact Cognates

Adjectives	Masculine Nouns El (ehl)	Feminine Nouns La (lah)
ambicioso (ahm-bee-see-yoh-soh)	aniversario (ah-nee-behr-sah-ree-yoh)	aspirina (ahs-pee-ree-nah)
confortable (kohn-fohr-tah-bleh)	automovíl (ow-toh-moh-beel)	bicicleta (bee-see-kleh-tah)
curioso (koo-ree-yoh-soh)	barbero (bahr-beh-roh)	blusa (bloo-sah)
delicioso (deh-lee-see-yoh-soh)	diccionario (deeks-yoh-nah-ree-yoh)	cathedral (kah-teh-drahl)
diferente (dee-feh rehn-teh)	elefante (eh-leh-fahn-teh)	dieta (dee-yeh-tah)

Adjectives	Masculine Nouns El (ehl)	Feminine Nouns La (lah)
elegante (eh-leh-gahn-teh)	grupo (groo-poh)	familia (fah-meel-yah)
excelente (ehk-seh-lehn-teh)	menú (meh-noo)	gasolina (gah-soh-lee-nah)
importante (eem-pohr-tahn-teh)	parque (pahr-keh)	guitarra (gee-tah-rrah)
imposible (eem-poh-see-bleh)	plato (plah-toh)	hamburguesa (ahm-boor-geh-sah)
moderno (moh-dehr-noh)	presidente (preh-see-dehn-teh)	lista (lees-tah)
necesario (neh-seh-sah-ree-yoh)	profesor (proh-feh-sohr)	música (moo-see-kah)
ordinario (ohr-dee-nah-ree-yoh)	programa (proh-grah-mah)	nacionalidad (nah-see-yoh-nah-lee-dahd)
posible (poh-see-bleh)	restaurante (rrehs-tow-rahn-teh)	opinión (oh-pee-nee-yohn)
probable (proh-bah-bleh)	salario (sah-lah-ree-yoh)	persona (pehr-soh-nah)
rico (rree-koh)	teléfono (teh-leh-foh-noh)	turista (too-rees-tah)
sincero (seen-seh-roh)	tigre (tee-greh)	universidad (oo-nee-behr-see-dahd)

Verbs

Verbs (action words) can be cognates, too. The majority of Spanish verbs fall into one of three categories: the -*ar* family, the -*er* family, and the -*ir* family. These verbs are considered regular because all verbs in the same family follow the same rules.

You should recognize the following verbs. Don't forget to add them to your growing list of cognates.

-ar Verbs	-er Verbs	-ir Verbs
acompañar (ah-kohm-pah-nyahr)	comprender (kohm-prehn-dehr)	aplaudir (ah-plow-deer)
celebrar (seh-leh-brahr)	responder (rrehs-pohn-dehr)	decidir (deh-see-deer)
declarar (deh-klah-rahr)	vender (behn-dehr)	describir (dehs-kree-beer)
entrar (ehn-trahr)		persuadir (pehr-swah-deer)
observar (ohb-sehr-bahr)		omitir (oh-mee-teer)
preparar (preh-pah-rahr)		recibir (rreh-see-beer)
usar (oo-sahr)		sufrir (soo-freer)

Chapter 2

Grammar in a Flash

In This Chapter

- Nouns
- Verbs
- Adjectives
- Adverbs
- Prepositions

If you really want to speak Spanish like a native, you will be happy to know that speaking a foreign language doesn't mean you have to mentally translate pages of rules. With today's communicative approach, it's simply not necessary for you to walk around with a dictionary under your arm. On the contrary, it means learning to use the language and its patterns naturally, the way a native speaker does. To do this, you need to know basic grammar as well as the idioms and colloquialisms used by native speakers.

Nouns for Naming

Nouns name people, places, things, or ideas. Just like in English, nouns can be replaced by pronouns (such as he, she, it, they). Unlike in English, however, all nouns in Spanish have a gender—a masculine or feminine designation. In Spanish, all nouns also have a number (singular or plural). Little articles (words that stand for "the" or "a") serve as noun identifiers and usually help indicate gender and number.

Don't worry: Even if you can't figure out the gender of a noun or if you use the wrong gender or number, you will still be understood as long as you use the correct word.

Gender

Gender is very easy in Spanish. All nouns that refer to males are masculine; those that refer to females are feminine. Use the noun identifiers in Table 2.1 to express "the" or "a":

Table 2.1   Singular Noun Identifiers

	the	**a, an, one**
Masculine	el	un
Feminine	la	una

Some noun endings make it extremely easy to determine the gender. In general, masculine nouns end in -o and feminine nouns end in -a. Table 2.2 provides a list of endings that can help make the job of gender identification easy.

Table 2.2   Gender Identification Made Easy

Masculine	Endings	Feminine	Endings
-o	carro	-a	fiesta
		-ión	porción
		-dad	oportunidad
		-tad	amistad
		-tud	juventud
		-umbre	costumbre
		-ie	serie

Something Extra

Some nouns can be either masculine or feminine depending on whether the speaker is referring to a male or female. Just change the article without changing the spelling of the noun:

el artista	*la artista*
el estudiante	*la estudiante*

Some nouns are always just masculine or just feminine, no matter the sex of the person to whom you are referring:

el bebé	*la persona*

Of course, there are always exceptions to the rule—just make sure you don't get lazy, sloppy, and over-confident. Keep the following exceptions in mind for future use:

- Masculine nouns that end in *-a:*

  el clima (ehl klee-mah), the climate

  el día (ehl dee-yah), the day

  el idioma (ehl ee-dee-yoh-mah), the language

  el mapa (ehl mah-pah), the map

  el problema (ehl proh-bleh-mah), the problem

  el programa (ehl proh-grah-mah), the program

  el telegrama (ehl teh-leh-grah-mah), the telegram

- Feminine nouns that end in *-o:*

  la mano (lah mah-noh), the hand

  la radio (lah rrah-dee-yoh), the radio

  la foto, short for *fotografía* (lah foh-toh), the photo

  la moto, short for *motocicleta* (lah moh-toh), the motorcycle

  *Note: el radio = *radio (thing),* while la radio = *radio (stations).*

Number

When a Spanish noun refers to more than one person, place, thing, or idea, it must be made plural—just like in English. Table 2.3 shows that it is not enough to simply change the noun. The identifying article must be made plural, too.

Table 2.3   Plural Articles

	the	some
Masculine	los	unos
Feminine	las	unas

Forming the plural of nouns in Spanish is really quite easy. All you have to do is add *-s* to a singular noun that ends in a vowel, and add *-es* to a singular noun that ends in a consonant.

el muchacho   los muchachos   el autor   los autores
la muchacha   las muchachas   la ciudad   las ciudades

Something Extra

No ending is added for nouns already ending in *-s*, except for nouns ending in *-és*:

el jueves   los jueves

BUT

el inglés   los ingleses

(accent dropped to maintain original stress)

¡Cuidado!

For nouns ending in *-z*, change the *z* to *c* before adding *-es*:

el pez   los peces
una actriz   unas actrices

Verbs in Action

Verbs are words that indicate actions or states of being. Verbs require a subject, whether it is expressed or implied. Subjects can be nouns or pronouns and, just like in English, they are given a person and a number, as shown in Table 2.4.

Table 2.4 Subject Pronouns

Person	Singular	Plural
first	yo (yoh), I	nosotros (noh-soh-trohs), we
		nosotras (noh-soh-trahs), we, all female
second	tú (too), you	vosotros (boh-soh-trohs), you
		vosotras (boh-soh-trahs), you, plural, all female
third	él (ehl), he	ellos (eh-yohs), they
	ella (eh-yah), she	ellas (eh-yahs), they
	usted (Ud.), (oo-stehd) you	ustedes (Uds.) (oo-steh-dehs), you

Subject pronouns are not used as often in Spanish as they are in English. This is because the verb ending usually quite clearly identifies the subject.

To speak about a group of women, use *nosotras* or *vosotras* or *ellas*. When speaking about a mixed group, always use the masculine plural—regardless of the number of males in the group.

Tú is used when speaking to a relative, a close friend, a child, or a pet. In all other instances, use the polite form *Ud.* The *vosotros* form is used primarily in Spain. In Spanish-speaking countries of the Americas, the *Uds.* form is used.

Verbs are generally shown as an infinitive, the basic "to" form of the verb: to live, to laugh, to love. An infinitive, whether in Spanish or in English, is the form of the verb before it has been conjugated. Conjugation refers to changing the ending of a verb so it agrees with the subject and shows tense (past, present, and so on). Verbs can be regular (most verbs with the same ending follow the same rules) or irregular (there are no rules, so you must memorize them).

The Present Tense

Regular verbs in Spanish belong to one of three large families: verbs whose infinitives end in *-ar*, *-er*, or *-ir*. The verbs within each family are conjugated in exactly the same manner. After you've learned the pattern for one family, you know all the regular verbs in that family.

The present tense is used …

- To express what generally happens all the time:

  Miro la televisión todas las noches.
  I watch television every night.

- To express events that are taking place at present:

  Mis amigos van al cine.
  My friends are going to the movies.

- To imply actions or events that will occur in the immediate future:

  Te veo mañana.
  I'll see you tomorrow.

- To express an action that began in the past and continues in the present if used with *hace* + length of time + *que:*

  Hace un año que estudio español.
  I've been studying Spanish for a year.

Table 2.5 shows how to conjugate regular verbs in the present tense.

Table 2.5 The Present Tense of Regular Verbs

Subject	-ar Verbs (hablar)	-er Verbs (comer)	-ir Verbs (abrir)
yo	hablo	como	abro
tú	hablas	comes	abres
el, ella, Ud.	habla	come	abre
nosotros	hablamos	comemos	abrimos
vosotros	habláis	coméis	abrís
ellos, ellas, Uds.	hablan	comen	abren

Verb Tables

Tables 2.6, 2.7, and 2.8 provide practical lists of the most frequently used *-ar*, *-er*, and *-ir* verbs. These are the ones you'll use the most in any given situation.

Table 2.6   Common -ar Verbs

Verb	Pronunciation	Meaning
acompañar	ah-kohm-pah-nyahr	to accompany
alquilar	ahl-kee-lahr	to rent
aterrizar	ah-tehr-ree-sar	to land
ayudar	ah-yoo-dahr	to help
buscar	boos-kahr	to look for
cambiar	kahm-bee-yahr	to change
comprar	kohm-prahr	to buy
desear	deh-seh-yahr	to desire
entrar	ehn-trahr	to enter
escuchar	ehs-koo-chahr	to listen (to)
estudiar	ehs-too-dee-yahr	to study
explicar	ehks-plee-kahr	to explain
firmar	feer-mahr	to sign
hablar	hahb-lahr	to speak, to talk
invitar	een-bee-tahr	to invite
lavar	lah-bahr	to wash
llegar	yeh-gahr	to arrive
mirar	mee-rahr	to look at
necesitar	neh-seh-see-tahr	to need
pagar	pah-gahr	to pay
pasar	pah-sahr	to spend (time)
preguntar	preh-goon-tahr	to ask
presentar	preh-sehn-tahr	to introduce
prestar	prehs-tahr	to lend
regresar	rreh-greh-sahr	to return
reparar	rreh-pah-rahr	to repair
reservar	rreh-sehr-bahr	to reserve

continues

continued

Verb	Pronunciation	Meaning
telefonear	teh-leh-foh-neh-yahr	to phone
terminar	tehr-mee-nahr	to end
tocar	toh-kahr	to touch
tomar	toh-mahr	to take
usar	oo-sahr	to use, to wear
viajar	bee-yah-hahr	to travel

Table 2.7 Common -er Verbs

Verb	Pronunciation	Meaning
aprender	ah-prehn-dehr	to learn
beber	beh-behr	to drink
comer	koh-mehr	to eat
comprender	kohm-prehn-dehr	to understand
creer	kreh-yehr	to believe
deber	deh-behr	to have to, to owe
leer	leh-yehr	to read
responder	rrehs-pohn-dehr	to respond
vender	behn-dehr	to sell

Table 2.8 Common -ir Verbs

Verb	Pronunciation	Meaning
abrir	ah-breer	to open
asistir	ah-sees-teer	to attend
decidir	deh-see-deer	to decide
describir	dehs-kree-beer	to describe

Verb	Pronunciation	Meaning
escribir	ehs-kree-beer	to write
recibir	rreh-see-beer	to receive
subir	soo-beer	to go up, to climb
vivir	bee-beer	to live

Something Extra

Go-go verbs are regular (in all other forms except yo) or irregular verbs whose yo form ends in -go instead of -o. The most common go-go verbs are these:

yo digo	I say, tell
yo hago	I make, do
yo oígo	I hear
yo pongo	I put
yo salgo	I leave
yo tengo	I have
yo traigo	I bring
yo valgo	I am worth
yo vengo	I come

"Shoe verbs" require a spelling change that works as if we put the subject pronouns that follow one set of rules within the shoe and the others outside the shoe. The shoe looks like this:

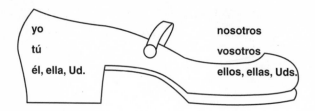

Note that these verbs have changes for all subject pronouns except *nosotros* and *vosotros*.

The changes occur as follows:

- Verbs ending in *-ar* and *-er:*

  The vowel in the stem makes the following change:

  e changes to *ie*

  | *pensar* (to think) | *yo pienso* | *nosotros pensamos* |
  | *querer* (to want) | *yo quiero* | *nosotros queremos* |

  o changes to *ue*

  | *mostrar* (to show) | *yo maestro* | *nosotros mostramos* |
  | *poder* (to be able to) | *yo puedo* | *nosotros podemos* |

- Verbs ending in *-ir:*

  The vowel in the stem makes the following change:

  e changes to *ie*

  | *preferir* (to prefer) | *yo prefiero* | *nosotros preferimos* |

o **changes to** *ue*

dormir   yo *duermo*   *nosotros dormimos*
(to sleep)

e **changes to** *i*

pedir   yo *pido*   *nosotros pedimos*
(to ask)

Something Extra

For verbs ending in *-uir* (but not *-guir*), insert a *y* after the *u* in all forms within the shoe:

yo incluyo	nosotros incluimos
tú incluyes	vosotros incluís
él incluye	ellos incluyen

Verbs ending in *-iar* and *-uar*, such as *guiar* (to guide), *enviar* (to send), and *variar* (to vary), require an accent in all forms except *nosotros*:

yo envío	nosotros enviamos
tú envías	vosotros enviáis
él envía	ellos envían

The Present Progressive

The present progressive expresses what a particular subject is doing right now, at this moment in time. The present progressive is formed by using the present tense form of the verb *estar* (to be) that corresponds to the subject. A gerund (in English, the *-ing* form of the verb) then follows immediately.

Gerunds are formed as follows:

- If the infinitive ends in -*ar*, drop -*ar* and add -*ando*:

  hablar (to speak)   *hablando*   speaking

  Están hablando español.
  They are speaking Spanish.

- If the infinitive ends in -*er* or -*ir*, drop the respective ending and add -*iendo*:

  beber (to drink)   *bebiendo*   drinking

  Estoy bebiendo té.
  I'm drinking tea.

  escribir (to write)   *escribiendo*   writing

  ¿Qué estás escribiendo?
  What are you writing?

Something Extra

If an -*er* or -*ir* verb has a stem ending in a vowel, add -*yendo* instead of -*endo*:

   leer (to read)   *leyendo* (reading)

   Está leyendo el periódico.
   He's reading the newspaper.

   oír (to hear)   *oyendo* (hearing)

   Estamos oyendo malas noticias.
   We're hearing bad news.

The Preterit (The Past Tense)

The preterit expresses an action or event that was begun or completed at a specific time in the past, even if the time isn't mentioned.

> *La película empezó a las ocho.*
> The film began at eight o'clock.
>
> *Me levanté temprano.*
> I got up early.

The preterit may also express an action or event that was repeated a stated number of times.

> *Fui a España tres veces.*
> I went to Spain three times.

To form the preterit of regular verbs, drop the infinitive ending (*-ar*, *-er*, *-ir*) and add the endings as illustrated in Table 2.9. Note that regular *-er* and *-ir* verbs have the same preterit endings.

Table 2.9   Forming the Preterit of Regular Verbs

	-ar Verbs usar (to use)	-er Verbs comer (to eat)	-ir Verbs abrir (to open)
yo	us**é**	com**í**	abr**í**
tú	us**aste**	com**iste**	abr**iste**
él	us**ó**	com**ió**	abr**ió**
nosotros	us**amos**	com**imos**	abr**imos**
vosotros	us**asteis**	com**isteis**	abr**isteis**
ellos	us**aron**	com**ieron**	abr**ieron**

¡Cuidado!

Verbs ending in *-car*, *-gar*, and *-zar* drop the *-ar* infinitive ending to form the preterit and have the following respective spelling changes in the *yo* form only:

c changes to *qu*	Yo lo busqué.	I looked for it.
g changes to *gu*	Yo pagué mucho.	I paid a lot.
z changes to *c*	Yo lo gocé.	I enjoyed it.

Most irregular Spanish verbs have the same preterit endings regardless of their infinitive endings. These endings are as follows:

yo	*-e*	*nosotros*	*-imos*
tú	*-iste*	*vosotros*	*-isteis*
él	*-o*	*ellos*	*-ieron*

¡Cuidado!

The irregular verbs *ir* (to go) and *ser* (to be) have the same preterit forms:

yo fui, tú fuiste, él fue, nosotros fuimos, vosotros fuisteis, ellos fueron

The following are high-frequency irregular verbs in the preterit:

Verb	Stem
andar (to walk)	anduv-
caber (to fit)	cup-
estar (to be)	estuv-
hacer (to make, do)	hic-, hiz- (for él, ella, and Ud.)
poder (to be able to)	pud-
querer (to want)	quis-
saber (to know)	sup-
tener (to have)	tuv-
venir (to come)	vin-

¡Cuidado!

The *-ieron* ending for irregular verbs becomes *-eron* before the letter *j*:

decir (to say)	*dij-*
producir (to produce)	*produj-*
traer (to bring)	*traj-*

Note the similar irregular preterit for the following verbs:

dar (to give): *di, diste, dio, dimos, disteis, dieron*

ver (to see): *vi, viste, vio, dimos, visteis, vieron*

The Imperfect

The imperfect expresses continuous or repeated actions, events, situations, or states in the past and is used …

- To describe what *was* or *used to* happen again and again in the past:

  Los niños jugaban.
  The children were playing.

  Todos los sábados yo iba al cine.
  Every Saturday I used to go to the movies.

- To express an ongoing past action:

  Elena trabajaba por la noche.
  Elena worked at night.

- To describe people, things, or time in the past:

  Su madre era muy bonita.
  His mother was very beautiful.

  La calle estaba desierta.
  The street was deserted.

  Eran las cinco de la tarde.
  It was 5 o'clock in the afternoon.

- To express a state of mind in the past with verbs such as *creer* (to believe), *pensar* (to think), *poder* (to be able to), *querer* (to want), and *saber* (to know):

  Ella pensaba ir de compras.
  She was thinking about going shopping.

- To describe a situation that was going on in the past when another action occurred:

  Yo salía cuando el teléfono sonó.
  I was going out when the telephone rang.

To form the imperfect of regular verbs, drop the infinitive ending (*-ar*, *-er*, *-ir*) and add the endings shown in Table 2.10. Note that the imperfect endings are the same for *-er* and *-ir* verbs.

Table 2.10   Forming the Imperfect

	-ar Verbs	-er Verbs	-ir Verbs
yo	-aba	-ía	-ía
tú	-abas	-ías	-ías
él	-aba	-ía	-ía
nosotros	-ábamos	-íamos	-íamos
vosotros	-abais	-íais	-íais
ellos	-aban	-ían	-ían

The three verbs that are irregular in the imperfect are shown in Table 2.11.

Table 2.11   Verbs Irregular in the Imperfect

	ir (to go)	ser (to be)	ver (to see)
yo	iba	era	veía
tú	ibas	eras	veías
él	iba	era	veía
nosotros	íbamos	éramos	veíamos
vosotros	ibais	erais	veíais
ellos	iban	eran	veían

The Future

The future can be expressed in three ways:

- By using the present to imply the future

  Ellos llegan esta noche.
  They are arriving tonight.

- By using *ir* (to go) + *a* + the infinitive of a verb

  Ellos van a llegar esta noche.
  They are going to arrive tonight.

- By using the future tense

  Ellos llegarán esta noche.
  They will arrive tonight.

The future tense is formed by adding the future endings to the infinitives of regular verbs as follows:

yo	-e	nosotros	-emos
tú	ás	vosotros	-éis
él	-á	ellos	-án

Ud. trabajará mañana.
You will work tomorrow.

Yo venderé mi coche pronto.
I will sell my car right away.

Ellos recibirán el paquete.
They will receive the package.

The following verbs have irregular stems in the future and, therefore, do not use the infinitive. To form the future, simply add the ending to the stems indicated:

caber	to fit	*cabr-*
decir	to say	*dir-*
hacer	to make	*har-*
poder	to be able	*podr-*
poner	to put	*pondr-*
querer	to want	*querr-*
saber	to know	*sabr-*
salir	to leave	*saldr-*
tener	to have	*tendr-*
valer	to be worth	*valdr-*
venir	to come	*vendr-*

The Conditional

The conditional is a mood that expresses what the subject *would* do or what *would* happen under certain circumstances.

The conditional is formed by adding the -*er* and -*ir* imperfect endings to the future stem of regular and irregular verbs as follows:

yo	-*ía*	*nosotros*	-*íamos*
tú	-*ías*	*vosotros*	-*íais*
él	-*ía*	*ellos*	-*ían*

¿Me hablaría?
Would he speak to me?

Diríamos la verdad.
We would tell the truth.

The Subjunctive

The subjunctive is a mood that expresses wishing, wanting, emotion, doubt, and uncertainty. Because the subjunctive is not a tense (a verb form indicating time), the present subjunctive is used to express actions in the present or future.

The subjunctive is used when the following conditions are met:

- There are two different clauses with two different subjects.
- The two clauses are joined by *que*.
- One of the clauses shows wishing, wanting, emotion, doubt, or uncertainty.

To form the subjunctive of regular verbs, drop the -*o* ending from the *yo* form of the present tense; for -*ar* verbs, add the -*er/-ir* present tense verb endings (-*e*, -*es*, -*e*, -*emos*, -*éis*, -*en*); and for -*er/-ir* verbs, add the -*ar* present tense verb endings (-*a*, -*as*, -*a*, -*amos*, -*áis*, -*an*).

> *Es importante que te hable.*
> It's important that I speak to you.
>
> *El profesor duda que él aprenda mucho.*
> The teacher doubts that he is learning much.
>
> *Es posible que ellas escriban esta carta.*
> It is possible that they will write this letter.

The following verbs with irregular present tense *yo* forms will also have irregular subjunctive forms with the *-ar* present tense verb endings:

conocer	to know	*conozc–*
decir	to say	*dig–*
hacer	to make, do	*hag–*
oír	to hear	*oig–*
poner	to put	*pong–*
salir	to go out	*salg–*
traer	to bring	*traig–*
venir	to come	*veng–*

¡Cuidado!

In all forms of the subjunctive:

For *-car* verbs, *c* changes to *que:*
  yo busque

For *-gar* verbs, *g* changes to *gu:*
  nosotros paguemos

For *-zar* verbs, *z* changes to *c:*
  ellos crucen

For stem-changing shoe verbs:

- Verbs ending in *-ar* and *-er* have the same stem changes in the subjunctive as they do in the present.

que yo piense	*que nosotros pensemos*
que tú vuelvas	*que vosotros volváis*

- Verbs ending in *-ir* have the same stem changes in the subjunctive for the *yo, tú, él,* and *ellos* forms, but change the *e* to *i* or *o* to *u* in the *nosotros* and *vosotros* forms.

que él sienta	*que nosotros sintamos*
que yo duerma	*que vosotros durmáis*
que tú pidas	*que nosotros pidamos*

Something Extra

To avoid using the subjunctive, you may use the correctly conjugated form of *tener* + *que* + the infinitive of a verb to express something that has to be done:

I have to work today.

> *Yo tengo que trabajar hoy.*

instead of

> *Es necesario que trabaje hoy.*

High-frequency irregular verbs used in the subjunctive include the following:

dar (to give): *dé, des, dé, demos, deis, den*

estar (to be): *esté, estés, esté, estemos, estéis, estén*

ir (to go): *vaya, vayas, vaya, vayamos, vayáis, vayan*

saber (to know): *sepa, sepas, sepa, sepamos, sepáis, sepan*

ser (to be): *sea, seas, sea, seamos, seáis, sean*

Adjectives at Work

Adjectives help to describe nouns. Unlike in English, in Spanish all adjectives agree in number and gender with the nouns they modify. In other words, in a Spanish sentence, all the words have to match. If the noun is singular, its adjective must also be singular. If the noun is feminine, you must be sure to give the correct feminine form of the adjective.

With most adjectives, you can form the feminine by simply changing the -*o* of the masculine form to an -*a*, as shown in Table 2.12.

Table 2.12   Forming Feminine Adjectives

Masculine	Pronun-ciation	Feminine	Meaning
alto	ahl-toh	alta	tall
bajo	bah-hoh	baja	short
bonito	boh-nee-toh	bonita	pretty
bueno	bweh-noh	buena	good
delicioso	deh-lee-see-yoh-soh	deliciosa	delicious
divertido	dee-behr-tee-doh	divertida	fun
feo	feh-yoh	fea	ugly
flaco	flah-koh	flaca	thin
gordo	gohr-doh	gorda	fat
malo	mah-loh	mala	bad
moreno	moh-reh-noh	morena	dark-haired

continues

Table 2.12   Forming Feminine Adjectives (continued)

Masculine	Pronun-ciation	Feminine	Meaning
nuevo	nweh-boh	nueva	new
pequeño	peh-keh-nyoh	pequeña	small
rico	rree-koh	rica	rich
rubio	rroo-bee-yoh	rubia	blond
simpático	seem-pah-tee-koh	simpática	nice
sincero	seen-seh-roh	sincera	sincere
tímido	tee-mee-doh	tímida	shy
viejo	bee-yeh-hoh	vieja	old

The adjectives in Table 2.13 end in -e, -ista, or a consonant. It is not necessary to make any changes to get the feminine form.

Table 2.13   Adjectives

Adjective	Pronunciation	Meaning
Adjectives ending in -e		
alegre	ah-leh-greh	happy
elegante	eh-leh-gahn-teh	elegant
excelente	ehks-seh-lehn-teh	excellent
grande	grahn-deh	big
importante	eem-pohr-tahn-teh	important
inteligente	een-teh-lee-hehn-teh	intelligent

Adjective	Pronunciation	Meaning
interesante	een-teh-reh-sahn-teh	interesting
pobre	poh-breh	poor
responsable	rrehs-pohn-sah-bleh	responsible
triste	trees-teh	sad

Adjectives ending in -ista

egoísta	eh-goh-ees-tah	selfish
optimista	ohp-tee-mees-tah	optimistic
pesimista	peh-see-mees-tah	pessimistic
realista	rree-yah-lees-tah	realistic

Adjectives ending in a consonant

cortés	kohr-tehs	courteous
cruel	kroo-ehl	cruel
difícil	dee-fee-seel	difficult
fácil	fah-seel	easy
joven	hoh-behn	young
popular	poh-poo-lahr	popular

In English, adjectives generally are placed before
the nouns they modify (for example, the tall man).
In Spanish, however, most adjectives come after the
nouns they describe (for example, *el hombre grande*).
Don't let this bother you. If you make a mistake,
you'll still be understood.

Adverbs in Use

Adverbs are words that describe verbs, adjectives, or other adverbs. In English, most adverbs end in *-ly* (for example, he dances slowly). In Spanish, they end in *-mente* (for example, *él baila rápidamente*).

¡Cuidado!

Masculine adjectives ending in *-or* add an *-a* to form the feminine:

encantador   *encantadora*

Adjectives showing nationality that end in a consonant add *-a* and may drop an accent to form the feminine:

inglés   *inglesa*

Something Extra

If you can't think of the adverb or if the adjective cannot be used with *mente*, you can use the preposition *con* + a noun:

con cuidado   *cuidadosamente* carefully

con paciencia *pacientemente*   patiently

To form adverbs, simply add *-mente* to the feminine, singular form of the adjective. Remember to look for the letter at the end of the adjective and pay attention to selecting the correct feminine form. Table 2.14 shows you how to do this.

Table 2.14 Adverbs Formed from Feminine Adjectives

Masculine	Feminine	Adverb	Meaning
completo	completa	completamente	completely
especial	especial	especialmente	especially
final	final	finalmente	finally
frecuente	frecuente	frecuentemente	frequently
lento	lenta	lentamente	slowly
rápido	rápida	rápidamente	quickly

Something Extra

When you find it necessary to describe an action with two or more adverbs, add *mente* only to the last one. The other adverbs should be shown in the feminine, singular adjective form. It is assumed that *mente* would have been added had they stood alone.

> *Enrique habla clara, lenta, fácil, y elocuentemente.*
>
> Henry speaks clearly, slowly, easily, and eloquently.

Prepositions

Prepositions show the relationship between a noun and another word in a sentence. Table 2.15 shows common prepositions you will find very useful.

Table 2.15 Prepositions

Preposition	Pronunciation	Meaning
a	ah	to, at
además de	ah-deh-mahs deh	in addition to
al lado de	ahl lah-doh deh	at the side of
alrededor (de)	ahl-reh-deh-dohr (deh)	around
antes (de)	ahn-tehs (deh)	before
cerca (de)	sehr-kah (deh)	near
con	kohn	with
contra	kohn-trah	against
de	deh	of, from, about
debajo (de)	deh-bah-hoh (deh)	under
delante (de)	deh-lahn-teh (deh)	in front (of)
dentro (de)	dehn-troh (deh)	within, inside of
después (de)	dehs-pwehs (deh)	after
detrás (de)	deh-trahs (deh)	behind, in back (of)
en	ehn	in, on, at
encima (de)	ehn-see-mah (deh)	above
enfrente de	ehn-frehn-teh deh	in front of, opposite, facing
entre	ehn-treh	between, among
en vez de	ehn behs deh	instead of

Preposition	Pronunciación	Meaning
frente a	frehn-teh ah	opposite, facing
fuera de	fweh-rah deh	outside of
hacia	ah-see-yah	toward
hasta	ahs-tah	up to, until
lejos (de)	leh-hohs (deh)	far (from)
para	pah-rah	for, in order to
por	pohr	by, through
según	seh-goon	according to
sin	seen	without
sobre	soh-breh	on, upon

¡Cuidado!

Contractions form with *a* and *de*,

$a + el = al$ $de + el = del$

Hablo al hombre. *Hablo del hombre.*
I speak *to* the I speak *about* the
man. man.

The following pronouns are used after prepositions:

mí	me	*nosotros(as)*	us
ti	you	*vosotros(as)*	you
él	him	*ellos*	them
ella	her	*ellas*	them
Ud.	you	*Uds.*	you

¡Cuidado!

Note how to express "with me" or "with you" (familiar):

conmigo   *contigo*

Getting Personal

In This Chapter

- Greetings and salutations
- *Ser* (to be) versus *estar* (to be)
- Professions
- Countries
- Family members
- Possession
- *Tener* (to have)
- Asking questions

The best way to learn a foreign language is to find a friend who is a sympathetic native speaker and then just jabber away. Talk about anything and everything that strikes your fancy. Ask to be helped and corrected. Don't be shy about using a dictionary or about asking for help with unfamiliar words. To develop a friendship, you have to talk about yourself and ask about your newfound friend.

Don't be shy. Strike up a conversation using some or all of the following phrases as your opening lines:

Spanish	Pronunciation	Meaning
Hola	oh-lah	Hello
Buenos días	bweh-nohs dee-yahs	Good morning
Buenas tardes	bweh-nahs tahr-dehs	Good afternoon
Buenas noches	bweh-nahs noh-chehs	Good evening
Señor	seh-nyohr	Sir
Señorita	seh-nyoh-ree-tah	Miss
Señora	seh-nyoh-rah	Mrs.
Me llamo ...	meh yah-moh	My name is ... (I call myself)
¿Cómo se llama?	koh-moh seh yah-mah	What is your name?
¿Cómo está Ud.?	koh-moh ehs-tah oo-stehd	How are you?
Muy bien	mwee byehn	Very well
Regular	rreh-goo-lahr	So-so
Así, así	ah-see ah-see	So-so

The Verbs "To Be": *Ser* and *Estar*

To ask and answer even the simplest questions in Spanish, you need to know the verbs that express "to be"—*ser* and *estar*. These verbs are irregular, and all of their forms must be memorized.

Ser

---

yo soy (soy)	nosotros somos (soh-mohs)
tú eres (eh-rehs)	vosotros sois (soys)
él, ella, Ud. es (ehs)	ellos, ellos, Uds. son (sohn)

1. **Expresses origin, nationality, basic traits, or and relatively permanent characteristics of the subject:**

    Soy de España.   *Soy americana.*   *Soy alto.*

    I'm from Spain.   I'm American.   I'm tall.

2. **Identifies a subject or its traits that will probably remain the same for a long period of time:**

    Mi padre es doctor.   My father is a doctor.

3. **Expresses times and dates:**

    Son las tres.   *Es el tres de mayo.*

    It's 3 o'clock.   It's May 3rd.

4. **Expresses possession:**

    Es mi coche.   *Es de Marta.*

    It's my car.   It's Martha's.

5. **Is used in impersonal expressions:**

    Es necesario estudiar. It's necessary to study.

Estar

---

yo estoy (ehs-toy)	nosotros estamos (ehs-tah-mohs)
tú estás (ehs-tahs)	vosotros estáis (ehs-tahys)
él, ella, Ud. está (ehs-tah)	ellos, ellas, Uds. están (ehs-tahn)

continues

continued

Estar

1. **Describes a condition or state that is generally temporary and may change.**
   Estoy cansado.   I'm tired.

2. **Expresses location:**
   El hotel está allá.   The hotel is there.

3. **Forms the progressive tenses (see Chapter 2):**
   Estoy escuchando.   I'm listening.

And What's Your Line of Work?

Use Table 3.1 to refer to your profession. To make a profession feminine, change the final *o* to *a*. If the profession ends in -*or*, add *a*. No change is necessary if the profession ends in -*a* or -*e*.

Table 3.1   Professions

Profession	Spanish	Pronunciation
accountant	contable (m. or f.)	kohn-tah-bleh
businessman/ woman	hombre/ mujer de negocios	ohm-breh/moo-hehr deh neh-goh-see-yohs
dentist	dentista (m. or f.)	dehn-tees-tah

Profession	Spanish	Pronunciation
doctor	doctor (m.)	dohk-tor
engineer	ingeniero	een-heh-nee-yeh-roh
firefighter	bombero	bohm-beh-roh
government employee	empleado del gobierno	ehm-pleh-yah-doh dehl goh-bee-yehr-noh
hairdresser	barbero	bahr-beh-roh
jeweler	joyero	hoh-yeh-roh
lawyer	abogado	ah-boh-gah-doh
nurse	enfermero	ehn-fehr-meh-roh
police officer	agente de policía (m.)	ah-hen-teh deh poh-lee-see-yah
postal worker	cartero	kahr-teh-roh
programmer	programador	proh-grah-mah-dohr
salesperson	vendedor	behn-deh-dohr
secretary	secretario	seh-kreh-tah-ree-yoh
student	estudiante (m. or f.)	ehs-too-dee-yahn-teh
teacher	profesor	proh-feh-sohr
waiter	camarero	kah-mah-reh-roh

Where Are You From?

Travelers usually are very curious to know where other travelers come from, especially if they detect a foreign accent. Use the verb *ser* + *de* + the name of your country to say where you are from. Table 3.2 will help you express yourself quite easily.

Table 3.2   Countries Around the World

Country	Spanish	Pronunciation
Canada	el Canadá	ehl kah-nah-dah
England	Inglaterra	een-glah-teh-rah
France	Francia	frahn-see-yah
Germany	Alemania	ah-leh-mah-nee-yah
Greece	Grecia	greh-see-yah
Ireland	Irlanda	eer-lahn-dah
Italy	Italia	ee-tahl-yah
Japan	el Japón	ehl hah-pohn
Norway	Noruega	nohr-oo-eh-gah
Russia	Rusia	rroo-see-yah
Spain	España	ehs-pah-nyah
Sweden	Suecia	soo-eh-see-yah
Switzerland	Suiza	soo-wee-sah
United States	los Estados Unidos	lohs ehs-tah-dohs oo-nee-dohs

And Now for the Loved Ones

No introductory conversation is complete without opening your wallet and showing photos of those you hold near and dear to your heart. Use Table 3.3 to identify everyone correctly.

Table 3.3   Family Members

Member	Pronunciation	Meaning
abuelo	ah-bweh-loh	grandfather
abuela	ah-bweh-lah	grandmother
padrino	pah-dree-noh	godfather
madrina	mah-dree-nah	godmother
padre	pah-dreh	father
madre	mah-dreh	mother
padastro	pah-dahs-troh	stepfather
madastra	mah-dahs-trah	stepmother
hijo	ee-hoh	son, male child
hija	ee-hah	daughter, female child
hermano	ehr-mah-noh	brother
hermana	ehr-mah-nah	sister
hermanastro	ehr-mah-nahs-troh	stepbrother
hermanastra	ehr-mah-nahs-trah	stepsister
primo	pree-moh	cousin
prima	pree-mah	cousin (female)
sobrino	soh-bree-noh	nephew
sobrina	soh-bree-nah	niece
tío	tee-yoh	uncle
tía	tee-yah	aunt
nieto	nee-yeh-toh	grandson
nieta	nee-yeh-tah	granddaughter
suegro	sweh-groh	father-in-law
suegra	sweh-grah	mother-in-law

continues

Table 3.3 Family Members (continued)

Member	Pronunciation	Meaning
yerno	yehr-noh	son-in-law
nuera	nweh-rah	daughter-in-law
cuñado	koo-nyah-doh	brother-in-law
cuñada	koo-nyah-dah	sister-in-law
novio	noh-bee-yoh	boyfriend
novia	noh-bee-yah	girlfriend

To express plurals, use the masculine plural form: *hijos* (children), *padres* (parents), *abuelos* (grandparents), *suegros* (in-laws).

Showing Possession

To show possession in English, we use 's or s' after a noun. There are no apostrophes in Spanish, however. To translate "Julio's mother" into Spanish, a speaker would have to say "the mother of Julio," which is "*la madre de Julio.*" The preposition *de* means "of " and is used to express possession or relationship.

Possessive adjectives also can be used to show possession, as shown in Table 3.5. A possessive adjective should agree with the item possessed, not the possessor.

Es mi tía.   *Son mis hijos.*
That's my aunt.   They are my sons.

Table 3.5   Possessive Adjectives

Used Before Masculine Nouns		Used Before Feminine Nouns		
Singular	Plural	Singular	Plural	English
mi	mis	mi	mis	my
tu	tus	tu	tus	your
su	sus	su	sus	his, her, your, its
nuestro	nuestros	nuestra	nuestras	our
vuestro	vuestros	vuestra	vuestras	your
su	sus	su	sus	their, your

The Verb "To Have": *Tener*

Perhaps you would like to discuss how many children you have or your age. You also might want to tell how you feel at a particular moment. The verb you will find most helpful in these situations is *tener* (to have). Like the verbs *ser* and *estar*, *tener* is an irregular verb. All its forms (as seen in Table 3.6) must be memorized. High-frequency idiomatic expressions that use *tener* can be found in Appendix A.

Table 3.6   Conjugating Tener (to Have)

Conjugated Form of Tener	Pronunciation	Meaning
yo tengo	tehn-goh	I have
tú tienes	tee-yeh-nehs	You have
él, ella, Ud. tiene	tee-yeh-neh	He, she, one has

continues

Table 3.6 Conjugating Tener (to Have) (continued)

Conjugated Form of Tener	Pronunciation	Meaning
nosotros tenemos	teh-neh-mohs	We have
vosotros tenéis	teh-neh-yees	You have
ellos, ellas, Uds. tienen	tee-yeh-nehn	They, you (pl.) have

Asking Yes or No Questions

If your Spanish isn't quite as perfect as you'd like, you'll probably be content to ask people simple yes or no questions. Besides, that way you won't look too nosy.

Intonation

The easiest way to show that you are asking a question is simply to change your intonation by raising your voice at the end of the sentence:

> *¿Eres americano?*
> Are you American?

Tags

Another simple way to ask a question is to add a tag such as *¿verdad?*, *¿no?*, or *¿está bien?* to the end of a statement. These tags can mean "really?," "isn't that so?," "is it?," "isn't it?," "are you?," "aren't you?," "do you?," "don't you?," "all right?," or "okay?" When writing in Spanish, put an upside-down question mark at the beginning of the question and a standard one at the end.

> *Eres americano, ¿verdad?* (*¿no?, ¿está bien?*)
>
> You're American, right? (isn't that so?, aren't you?)

Inversion

Inversion means reversing the word order of the subject or subject pronoun and the conjugated verb form.

> *¿Eres tú americano?*

Asking for More Detailed Information

If you're anything like me, a simple yes or no answer never suffices. Use the questions in Table 3.7 to get all the information you want.

Table 3.7 Information Questions

Word/Phrase	Pronunciation	Meaning
adónde	ah-dohn-deh	to where
a qué hora	ah keh oh-rah	at what time
a quién	ah kee-yehn	to whom
a qué	ah keh	to what
con quién	kohn kee-yehn	with whom
con qué	kohn keh	with what

continues

Table 3.7 Information Questions

Word/Phrase	Pronunciation	Meaning
cuál	kwahl	which
de quién	deh kee-yehn	of, about, from whom, whose
de qué	deh keh	of, about, from what
cuánto(s)	kwahn-toh(s)	how much, many
cómo	koh-moh	how
dónde	dohn-deh	where
de dónde	deh dohn-deh	from where
por qué	pohr keh	why
cuándo	kwahn-doh	when
quién	kee-yehn	who, whom
qué	keh	what

The easiest way to ask for information is to put the question word immediately before the verbal phrase or thought.

| *¿Con quién viaja Ud.?* | With whom are you traveling? |

¿Qué? asks "what?" when referring to a description, a definition, or an explanation and asks "which?" when used before a noun.

¿Qué es esto?	What's that?
¿Qué estás comiendo?	What are you eating?
¿Qué programa estás mirando?	Which program are you watching?

¿Cuál? and *¿Cuáles?* generally ask "which?" They ask
"what?" before the verb *ser* (to be), except when asking
for the definition of a word (when *¿qué?* is used). They
ask "which (one)?" before the preposition *de*.

*¿**Cuál** es su nombre?*	*¿**Cuáles** quieres?*
What's your name?	Which (ones) do you want?
*¿**Cuál** de los dos prefieres?*	Which (one) of the two do you prefer?

In Spanish, all words that ask questions have accent
marks. This distinguishes them from words that are
spelled the same but that state information rather
than asking for it.

*¿**Dónde** vives?*	*Yo no sé donde tú vives.*
Where do you live?	I don't know where you live.

Something Extra _____

When followed by a noun, *cuánto* is
used as an adjective and must agree in
number and gender with the noun:

¿Cuánto dinero tienes?
How much money do you have?

¿Cuántas muchachas están cantando?
How many girls are singing?

Chapter 4

At the Airport

In This Chapter

- On the airplane and in the airport
- Travel by plane
- All about *ir* (to go)
- Giving and receiving directions
- What to say when you don't understand

Many people are all too well aware that a plane ride can be long and tedious. At times, you might experience minor inconveniences or delays for a wide variety of reasons. During your trip, you might want to change your seat or perhaps ask the flight crew some typical tourist questions. No doubt, if you are traveling on a foreign airline, you might find it helpful to use your knowledge of the language to help you get all the information you need. The terms in Table 4.1 will help you face any problem you might have.

Table 4.1 On the Inside

In-Plane Term	Spanish	Pronunciation
aisle	el pasillo	ehl pah-see-yoh
to board	abordar	ah-bohr-dahr
by the window	junto a la ventana	hoon-toh ah lah behn-tah-nah
crew	el equipo	ehl eh-kee-poh
to deplane, to exit	salir	sah-leer
emergency exit	la salida de emergencia	lah sah-lee-dah deh eh-mehr-hehn-see-yah
exit	la salida	lah sah-lee-dah
landing	el aterrizaje	ehl ah-teh-rree-sah-heh
life vest	el chaleco salvavidas	ehl chah-leh-koh sahl-bah-bee-dahs
(non) smokers	(no) fumadores	(noh) foo-mah-doh-rehs
on the aisle	en el pasillo	ehn ehl pah-see-yoh
row	la fila	lah fee-lah
seat	el asiento	ehl ah-see-yehn-toh
seat belt	el cinturón de seguridad	ehl seen-too-rohn deh seh-goo-ree-dahd
to smoke	fumar	foo-mahr
take off	el despegue	ehl dehs-peh-geh
trip	el viaje	ehl bee-yah-heh

The Eagle Has Landed

After you've landed, there should be plenty of signs to point you in the right direction. Where should you go first? You know it will take your bags a while to be unloaded. Do you need to use the bathroom? How about some foreign currency? After a delicious airline repast, do you still crave something to eat? Table 4.2 provides all the words you need to know when you are inside the airport.

Table 4.2   At the Airport

Place	Spanish	Pronunciation
airline	la aerolínea	lah ah-eh-roh-lee-neh-yah
airplane	el avión	ehl ah-bee-yohn
airport	el aeropuerto	ehl ah-eh-roh-pwehr-toh
arrival	la llegada	lah yeh-gah-dah
baggage claim area	el reclamo de equipaje	ehl rreh-klah-moh deh eh-kee-pah-heh
bathrooms	los baños	lohs bah-nyohs
bus stop	la parada de autobúses	lah pah-rah-dah deh ow-toh-boos-sehs
car rental	el alquiler de carros	ehl ahl-kee-lehr deh kah-rrohs
cart	el carrito	ehl kah-rree-toh
counter	el mostrador	ehl mohs-trah-dohr
customs	la aduana	lah ah-dwah-nah
departure	la salida	lah sah-lee-dah
elevators	los ascensores	lohs ah-sehn-soh-rehs

continues

Table 4.2 At the Airport (continued)

Place	Spanish	Pronunciation
entrance	la entrada	lah ehn-trah-dah
exit	la salida	lah sah-lee-dah
flight	el vuelo	ehl bweh-loh
gate	la puerta	lah pwehr-tah
information	informaciónes	een-fohr-mah-see-yoh-nehs
lost and found	la oficina de objetos perdidos	lah oh-fee-see-nah deh ohb-heh-tohs pehr-dee-dohs
to miss the flight	perder el vuelo	pehr-dehr ehl bweh-loh
money exchange	el cambio de dinero	ehl kahm-bee-yoh deh dee-neh-roh
porter	el portero	ehl pohr-teh-roh
stopover	la escala	lah ehs-kah-lah
suitcase	la maleta	lah mah-leh-tah
ticket	el boleto	ehl boh-leh-toh

Taking a Side Trip by Plane

If you intend to travel throughout the country or the continent by plane, the following phrases will prove useful:

> When is there a flight to ...?
> *¿Cuando hay un vuelo a ...?*
> kwahn-doh ahy oon bweh-loh ah

I would like a round-trip (one-way) ticket.
Quisiera un billete de ida y vuelta (sencillo).
kee-see-yeh-rah oon bee-yeh-teh deh ee-dah
ee bwel-tah (sehn-see-yoh)

I would like a seat next to the window (on the aisle).
Quisiera un asiento junto a la ventana (al pasillo).
kee-see-yeh-rah oon ah-syehn-toh hoon-to ah
lah behn-tah-nah (ahl pah-see-yoh)

What is the fare?
¿Cual es la tarifa?
kwahl ehs lah tah-ree-fah

Are meals served?
¿Se sirven comidas?
seh seer-behn koh-mee-dahs

When does the flight leave (arrive)?
¿Cuándo sale (llega) el vuelo?
kwahn-doh sah-leh (yeh-gah) ehl bweh-loh

Is it going to leave (arrive) on time (late)?
¿Va a salir (llegar) puntual (con retraso)?
bah ah sah-leer (yeh-gahr) poon-too-wahl
(kohn rreh-trah-soh)

I have only carry-on baggage.
Tengo solo equipaje de mano.
tehn-goh soh-loh eh-kee-pah-heh deh mah-noh

I'd like to check my bags.
Quisiera facturar mis maletas.
kee-see-yeh-rah fahk-too-rahr mees mah-leh-tas

At Security

If you have any problems getting through airport security, the following phrases will come in handy:

Here is my ticket and my passport.
Aquí tiene mi billete y mi pasaporte.
ah-kee tee-yeh-neh mee bee-yeh-teh ee mee pah-sah-pohr-teh

Do I have to remove my shoes (coat, belt)?
¿Tengo que quitarme los zapatos (el abrigo, el cinturón)?
tehn-goh keh kee-tahr-meh lohs zah-pah-tohs (ehl ah-bree-goh, elh seen-too-rrohn)

Will the scanner damage my film (camera, laptop)?
¿Va a dañar mis carretes (mi cámara, mi ordenador portátil el escáner)?
bah ah dah-nyahr mees kah-rreh-tehs (mee kah-mah-rah, mee ohr-deh-nah-dohr pohr-tah-teel ehl ehs-kah-nehr)

I have a medical condition. Here is a note (prescription) from my doctor.
Tengo una enfermedad. Aquí tiene una nota (receta) de mi médico.
tehn-goh oo-nah ehn-fehr-meh-dahd ah-kee tee-yeh-neh una noh-tah (rreh-she-tah) deh mee meh-dee-koh

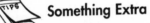

> ### Something Extra
>
> It's easy to get lost in sprawling international airports. To get yourself back on track, you need to know how to ask the correct questions. The following question will help you the most:
>
> *¿Dónde está + singular noun?*
> *¿Dónde está la salida?*
> Where's the exit?
>
> *¿Dónde están + plural noun?*
> *¿Dónde están los baños?*
> Where are the bathrooms?

The Verb "To Go": *Ir*

One verb that will really come in handy when traveling is shown in Table 4.3. *Ir* (to go) is an irregular verb that must be memorized.

Table 4.3   Conjugating Ir (to Go)

Conjugated Form of Ir	Pronunciation	Meaning
yo voy	boy	I go
tú vas	bahs	you go
él, ella, Ud. va	bah	he, she, you go(es)
nosotros vamos	bah-mohs	we go
vosotros vais	bahys	you go
ellos, ellas, Uds. van	bahn	they, you (pl.) go

Something Extra

Use *ir + a* to express going to a city, state, or country, as follows:

Voy a Nueva York.
I'm going to New York.

Use *ir + en* to express the many different ways to go someplace, as follows:

Voy a Nueva York en avión
I'm going to New York by plane.

Note the exception: *a pie,* on foot.

Voy al cine a pie.
I'm walking (going on foot) to the movies.

Complications

If the place you want to go is not within pointing distance, you'll need other directions. The verbs in Table 4.4 can help you get where you want to go or can help you aid someone else who is lost.

¡Cuidado!

Use either *Ud.* (singular) or *Uds.* (plural) as the subject of your command. Using the subject pronoun after the verb is optional. To make the command negative, simply put *no* before the verb.

Tome (Ud.) el coche.
Take the car.

No crucen (Uds.) la calle.
Don't cross the street.

Table 4.4 Giving Directions

Verb	Pronunciation	Meaning
baje(n)	bah-heh(n)	go down
camine(n)	kah-mee-neh(n)	walk
continúe(n)	kohn-tee-noo-weh(n)	continue
cruce(n)	kroo-seh(n)	cross
doble(n)	doh-bleh(n)	turn
pase(n)	pah-seh(n)	pass
sea(n)	seh-yah(n)	be
siga(n)	see-gah(n)	follow, continue
suba(n)	soo-bah(n)	go up
tenga(n)	tehn-gah(n)	have
tome(n)	toh-meh(n)	take
vaya(n)	bah-yah(n)	go

Por Versus Para

The Spanish words *por* and *para* can both mean "for." Consequently, there is often much confusion about when to use each. You should keep in mind the following rules:

Por Indicates	Para Indicates
motion	destination to a place
Paso por *la salida.*	*El avión sale* para *Cuba.*
I pass by the exit.	The airplane leaves for Cuba.

continues

continued

Por Indicates	Para Indicates
means, manner *Viajo* por *taxi.* I travel by taxi.	destination to a recipient *Este regalo es* para *mi amigo.* This gift is for my friend.
a period of time *Duermo* por *la noche.* I sleep at night.	a time limit *La cita es* para *el martes.* The appointment is for Tuesday.
frequency, in exchange for *Salgo una vez* por *mes.* I go out once a month.	purpose *Es un billete* para *el tren.* It's a ticket for the train.
Son dos plumas por *$20.* They are two pens for $20.	

What Did You Say?

What if someone gives you directions and you don't understand? Don't be embarrassed. The phrases in Table 4.5 can be a valuable aid if you need to have something repeated or if you need more information.

Table 4.5 When You Don't Understand

Expression	Pronunciation	Meaning
Con permiso	kohn pehr-mee-soh	Excuse me
Perdóneme	pehr-doh-neh-meh	Excuse me
Yo no comprendo	yoh noh kohm-prehn-doh	I don't understand

Expression	Pronunciation	Meaning
Yo no entiendo	yoh noh ehn-tee-yehn-doh	I don't understand
Yo no te oigo	yoh noh teh oy-goh	I don't hear you
Repita por favor	rreh-pee-tah pohr fah-bohr	Please repeat it
Otra vez	oh-trah behs	One more time/again
Hable más despacio	hah-bleh mahs dehs-pah-see-yoh	Speak more slowly
¿Qué dijo?	keh dee-hoh	What did you say?

Chapter 5

Traveling to Your Destination

In This Chapter

- Means of transportation
- Cardinal numbers
- Telling time
- Time expressions

If you're traveling in a Spanish-speaking country, several different means of transportation can get you to your destination. Consider the following: Are you traveling light? If so, you might want to mingle with people and take buses, subways, and trains. How tight is your budget and how much time do you have? If money is no object or if you're in a hurry, a taxi might be your best option. Do you enjoy seeing the countryside? If you're confident and are familiar with traffic laws and street signs, you might just want to rent a car.

Here's how to say how you're getting there:

Yo tomo ... (yoh toh-moh)   I'm taking ...

English	Spanish	Pronunciation
the boat	el barco	ehl bahr-koh
the bus	el autobús	ehl ow-toh-boos
the car	el coche	ehl koh-cheh
the car	el automóvil	ehl ow-toh-moh-beel
the car	el carro	ehl kah-rroh
the subway	el metro	ehl meh-troh
the taxi	el taxi	ehl tahk-see
the train	el tren	ehl trehn

If You're Traveling by Bus

The bus system in Madrid is efficient and inexpensive. A bus stop (*una parada de autobús*) is clearly marked by numbers. Transfers are not free (but bus service is quite inexpensive). Buses don't stop automatically; they must be hailed. A free bus map (*un plano de la red*) can easily be obtained at major tourist attractions and hotels.

In Mexico City, the buses tend to be very crowded and are more expensive than the subway. The routes go all over town and tend to be confusing.

Where is the nearest bus stop?
¿Dónde está la parada de autobús más cercana?
dohn-deh ehs-tah lah pah-rah-dah deh ow-toh-boos mahs sehr-kah-nah

How much is the fare?
¿Cuánto cuesta el billete?
kwahn-toh kwehs-tah ehl bee-yeh-teh

Do I need exact change?
¿Necesito cambio exacto?
neh-seh-see-toh kahm-bee-yoh ehk-sahk-toh

If You're Traveling by Subway

The subway systems in Madrid and Barcelona can boast of their cleanliness, comfort, safety, and economy. The 11 metro lines in Madrid are easily distinguishable on maps by numbers and different colors. *Un plan del metro*, a subway map, can be conveniently obtained for free at metro stops, hotels, department stores, and tourist offices. The sign *"Correspondencia"* indicates that free transfers and connections are available. If you don't exit, you can transfer as often as you like on just one ticket. Navigating the metro is easy—just look at the name of the last stop in the direction you want to go, and then follow the signs indicating that station.

Buenos Aires and Mexico City also have very clean and efficient subway systems.

Where is the nearest subway?
¿Dónde está la estación de metro más cercana?
dohn-deh ehs-tah lah ehs-tah-see-yohn deh
meh-troh mahs sehr-kah-nah

Where can I buy a ticket?
¿Dónde puedo comprar un billete?
dohn-deh pweh-doh kohm-prahr oon bee-yeh-teh

How much is the fare?
¿Cuánto es la tarifa?
kwahn-toh ehs lah tah-ree-fah

How many more stops are there?
¿Hay cuántas paradas más?
ahy kwahn-tahs pah-rah-dahs mahs

What's the next station?
¿Cuál es la prómixa estación?
kwahl ehs lah prohk-see-mah ehs-tah-see-yohn

Where is there a map?
¿Dónde hay un mapa?
dohn-deh ahy oon mah-pah

If You're Traveling by Taxi

Always try to take a metered taxi so you know exactly what fare to expect. Surcharges are imposed for luggage and night and holiday fares. *Un gran turismo* is an unmetered public-service taxi that charges higher rates. Remember to ask for the fare in advance if this is your choice. In Mexico City, orange-colored taxis generally are privately owned and can be called in advance; yellow cabs cruise for passengers. *Un colectivo* is a van or car that can be shared with other travelers going in the same general direction.

Where is the nearest taxi stand?
¿Dónde está la parada de taxi más cercana?
dohn-deh ehs-tah lah pah-rah-dah deh tahk-see mahs sehr-kah-nah

Would you please call me a cab?
¿Puede Ud. conseguirme un taxi, por favor?
pweh-deh oo-stehd kohn-seh-geer-meh oon
tahk-see pohr fah-bohr

I want to go …
Quiero ir …
kee-yeh-roh eer

Stop here.
Pare aquí.
pah-reh ah-kee

How much is it to …?
¿Cuánto cuesta hasta …?
kwahn-toh kwehs-tah ahs-tah …

Wait for me.
Espéreme.
ehs-peh-reh-meh

If You're Going by Train

If you're visiting Spain, Red Nacional de Ferro-
carriles Españoles (RENFRE) is the national rail-
road network of the country and is comparable to
AMTRAK in the United States. Spain has the most
inexpensive train fares in Europe. American travelers can only purchase a Eurail Pass in the United
States: they are unavailable outside the country. A
Eurail pass is a terrific bargain because it permits
unlimited travel rights throughout Europe. The
price of this card varies according to the number of
travel days you choose: 15, 25, 40, 60, or 90.

Where is the nearest train station?
¿Dónde está la estacíon de tren más cercana?
dohn-deh ehs-tah lah ehs-tah-see-yohn deh
trehn mahs sehr-kah-nah

I would like …
Quisiera …
kee-see-yeh-rah

> a first (second) class ticket.
> *un billete de primera (segunda) clase.*
> oon bee-yeh-teh deh pree-meh-rah
> (seh-goon-dah) klah-seh

> a round-trip ticket.
> *un billete de ida y vuelta.*
> oon bee-yeh-teh deh ee-dah ee bwehl-tah

> a (non) smoking compartment.
> *un departamento para (no) fumadores.*
> oon deh-pahr-tah-mehn-toh pah-rah (noh)
> foo-mah-doh-rehs

Is it a local (express)?
¿Es un tren local (un rápido)?
ehs oon trehn loh-kahl (oon rrah-pee-doh)

From what platform does it leave?
¿De qué andén sale?
deh keh ahn-dehn sah-leh

If You're Traveling by Car

So you're daring enough to go to *un alquiler de coches* to rent a car. Good for you! Always compare rates before you make a final choice. Don't be surprised when the price at the gas pump is almost double what you generally pay back home.

I'd like to rent a (give make of car).
Quiero alquilar un _____.
kee-yeh-roh ahl-kee-lahr oon

I prefer automatic transmission.
Prefiero el cambio automático.
preh-fee-yeh-roh ehl kahm-bee-yoh ow-toh-mah-tee-koh

How much does it cost per day (per week) (per kilometer)?
¿Cuánto cuesta por día (por semana) (por kilómetro)?
kwahn-toh kwehs-tah pohr dee-yah (pohr seh-mah-nah) (por kee-loh-meh-troh)

How much is the insurance?
¿Cuánto es el seguro?
kwahn-toh ehs ehl seh-goo-roh

Is the gas included?
¿Está incluída la gasolina?
ehs-tah een-kloo-eee-dah lah gah-soh-lee-nah

Do you accept credit cards? Which ones?
¿Acepta Ud. tarjetas de crédito? ¿Cuáles?
ah-sehp-tah oo-stehd tahr-heh-tahs deh kreh-dee-toh kwah-lehs

Do you fill it up with gas?
¿Lo llena Ud. con gasolina?
loh yeh-nah oo-stehd kohn gah-soh-lee-nah

¡Cuidado!

If you decide to rent a car, open the trunk and make sure there is a jack—*un gato* (oon gah-toh)—and a spare tire—*una goma de repuesto* (oo-nah goh-mah deh rrehs-pwehs-toh).

In Europe, distance is measured in kilometers. Table 4.4 shows the approximate equivalents.

Table 5.1   Distance Measures (Approximate)

Miles	Kilometers
.62	1
3	5
6	10
12	20
31	50
62	100

Heading in the Right Direction

By all means, learn your destination's road signs—some are not as obvious as they should be. You also need to know your compass directions.

Meaning	Direction	Pronunciation
to the north	al norte	ahl nohr-teh
to the east	al este	ahl ehs-teh
to the south	al sur	ahl soor
to the west	al oeste	ahl oh-wehs-teh

Familiarize yourself with the following before you venture out on your own in a car.

What's Your Number?

To tell someone which flight or bus you are taking or to figure out how much a rental car is going to set you back, you need to learn the Spanish numbers listed in Table 5.2. These numbers will also come in handy when you want to tell time, to count money, or to reveal your age.

Table 5.2 Cardinal Numbers

No.	Spanish	Pronun-ciation	No.	Spanish	Pronun-ciation
0	cero	seh-roh	19	diez y nueve	dee-yehs ee noo-eh-beh
1	uno	oo-noh	20	veinte	behn-teh
2	dos	dohs	21	veinti-uno	behn-tee-oo-noh
3	tres	trehs	22	veinti-dós	behn-tee dohs
4	cuatro	kwah-troh			
5	cinco	seen-koh	30	treinta	trehn-tah
6	seis	seh-yees	40	cuarenta	kwah-rehn-tah
7	siete	see-yeh-teh	50	cincuenta	seen-kwehn-tah
8	ocho	oh-choh			
9	nueve	noo-weh-beh	60	sesenta	seh-sehn-tah
10	diez	dee-yehs	70	setenta	seh-tehn-tah
11	once	ohn-seh	80	ochenta	oh-chen-tah
12	doce	doh-seh	90	noventa	noh-behn-tah
13	trece	treh-seh			
14	catorce	kah-tohr-seh	100	ciento	see-yehn-toh
15	quince	keen-seh			
16	diez y seis	dee-yehs ee seh-yees	101	ciento uno	see-yehn-toh oo-noh
17	diez y siete	dee-yehs ee see-yeh-teh	200	dos-cientos	dohs-see-yehn-tohs
18	diez y ocho	dee-yehs ee oh-choh	500	quini-entos	kee-nee-yehn-tohs

No.	Spanish	Pronun-ciation	No.	Spanish	Pronun-ciation
700	seteci-entos	seh-teh-see-yehn-tohs	2,000	dos mil	dohs meel
			100,000	cien mil	see-yehn meel
900	noveci-entos	noh-beh-see-yehn-tohs	1,000,000	un mil-lón	oon meel-yohn
1,000	mil	meel	2,000,000	dos mil-lones	dohs meel-yoh-nehs

Something Extra

The Spanish write the number 1 with a little hook on top. To distinguish a 1 from a 7, they put a line through the 7, as in 7.

In numerals and decimals, wherever we use commas, the Spanish use periods (and vice versa).

English	Spanish
1,000	1.000
.25	0,25
$9.95	$9,95

Spanish numbers are not too tricky. Look carefully again at Table 5.2, however, to pick up the following pointers:

- The conjunction *y* (and) is used only for numbers between 16 and 99.

● *Uno* is used only when counting. It becomes *un* before a masculine noun and *una* before a feminine noun.

uno, dos, tres ...
one, two, three ...

treinta y un muchachos
thirty-one boys

un hombre y una mujer
a man and woman

veinte y una muchachas
twenty-one girls

● The numbers 16 through 19 and 21 through 29 are generally written as one word. When this is done, the numbers 16, 22, 23, and 26 have accents:

16 *dieciséis*	22 *veintidós*
17 *diecisiete*	23 *veintitrés*
21 *veintiuno*	26 *veintiséis*

● Compounds of *ciento* (*doscientos, trescintos*) should agree with a feminine noun.

doscientos hombres two hundred men
trescientas mujeres three hundred women

● *Ciento* becomes *cien* before nouns and before the numbers *mil* and *millones*. Before all other numbers, *ciento* is used.

cien libros one hundred books
cien mil personas one hundred thousand people

cien veinte carros one hundred twenty cars
cien millones de dólare one billion dollars

- Although it is not used before *ciento* or *mil*, *un* is used before *millón*. If a noun follows *millón*, put *de* between *millón* and the noun.

cien pesetas	100 pesetas
un millón de habitantes	1,000,000 inhabitants
mil quinientos años	1,500 years

Do You Have the Time?

Now that you have the hang of Spanish numbers, it should be rather easy to express the time, as explained in Table 5.3.

What time is it?	At what time?
¿Qué hora es?	*¿A qué hora?*
keh oh-rah ehs	ah keh oh-rah

Table 5.3   Time

English	Spanish	Pronunciation
It is 1:00.	Es la una.	ehs lah oo-nah
It is 2:05.	Son las dos y cinco.	sohn lahs dohs ee seeng-koh
It is 3:10.	Son las tres y diez.	sohn lahs trehs y dee-yehs
It is 4:15.	Son las cuatro y cuarto.	sohn lahs kwah-troh ee kwahr-toh
It is 5:20.	Son las cinco y veinte.	sohn lahs seegn-koh ee behn-teh
It is 6:25.	Son las seis y veinticinco.	sohn lahs seh-yees -ee behn-tee-seen-koh

continues

Table 5.3 Time (continued)

English	Spanish	Pronunciation
It is 7:30.	Son las siete y media.	sohn lahs see-yeh-teh ee meh-dee-yah
It is 7:35 (25 min. to 8).	Son las ocho menos veinte y cinco.	sohn lahs oh-choh meh-nohs behn-teh-ee seen-koh
It is 8:40 (20 min. to 9).	Son las nueve menos veinte.	sohn lahs noo-weh-beh meh-nohs behn-teh
It is 9:45 (15 min. to 10).	Son las diez menos cuarto.	sohn lahs dee-yehs meh-nohs kwahr-toh
It is 10:50 (10 min. to 11).	Son las once menos diez.	sohn lahs ohn-seh meh-nohs dee-yehs
It is 11:55 (5 min. to 12).	Son las doce menos cinco.	sohn lahs doh-seh meh-nohs seen-koh
It is noon.	Es el mediodía.	ehs ehl meh-dee-yoh-dee-yah
It is midnight.	Es la media-noche.	ehs lah meh-dee-yah-noh-cheh

When telling time, make sure you do the following:

- Use *es* for "it is" when saying it is 1 o'clock. Use *son* for other numbers because they are plural.

- Use the hour + *y* + the number of minutes to express the time after the hour.

- Use the hour + *menos* + the number of minutes before that hour whenever it is more than half past the hour.

  Son las tres menos cuarto.
  It's 2:45.

It also is not unusual to hear the time
expressed as follows:

Son las dos y cuarenta y cinco.
It's 2:45.

It's not enough to know how to say what the time is.
You might want to know at what time an activity is
planned or whether it is taking place in the morning,
the afternoon, or the evening. The expressions in
Table 5.4 will help you deal with time.

Table 5.4   Time Expressions

Expression	Spanish	Pronunciation
a second	un segundo	oon seh-goon-doh
a minute	un minuto	oon mee-noo-toh
an hour	una hora	oo-nah oh-rah
in the morning (a.m.)	de la mañana	deh lah mah-nyah-nah
in the afternoon (p.m.)	de la tarde	deh lah tahr-deh
in the evening (p.m.)	de la noche	deh lah noh-cheh
at what time	a qué hora	ah keh oh-rah
at exactly 1:00	a la una en punto	ah lah oo-nah ehn poon-toh
at exactly 2:00	a las dos en punto	ah lahs dohs ehn poon-toh
at about 2:00	a eso de las dos	ah eh-soh deh lahs dohs

continues

Table 5.4 Time Expressions (continued)

Expression	Spanish	Pronunciation
a quarter of an hour	un cuarto de hora	oon kwahr-toh deh oh-rah
a half hour	media hora	meh-dee-yah oh-rah
in an hour	en una hora	ehn oo-nah oh-rah
until 2:00	hasta las dos	ahs-tah lahs dohs
before 3:00	antes de las tres	ahn-tehs deh lahs trehs
after 3:00	después de las tres	dehs-pwehs deh lahs trehs
since what time	desde qué hora	dehs-deh keh oh-rah
since 6:00	desde las seis	dehs-deh lahs seh-yees
an hour ago	hace una hora	ah-seh oo-nah oh-rah
per hour	por hora	pohr oh-rah
early	temprano	tehm-prah-noh
late	tarde	tahr-deh
late (in arriving)	en retraso	ehn rreh-trah-soh
on time	a tiempo	ah tee-yehm-poh
see you later	hasta luego	ahs-tah loo-weh-goh
see you soon	hasta la vista	ahs-tah lah bees-tah
see you tomorrow	hasta mañana	ahs-tah mah-nyah-nah
good-bye	adiós	ah-dee-yohs

Chapter 6

Money to Burn

In This Chapter

- Banking terms and expressions
- Banking transactions
- Different currencies

Need to exchange some money? Banks tend to give a favorable rate of exchange, but you may do even better at the ATM machine, which gives better rates than the bank, or at a *casa de cambio* (money exchange). Avoid changing money at the airport, the train station, or at your hotel, where the rates are generally quite unfavorable.

Perhaps you have greater goals, however. Maybe you want to purchase real estate, set up a business, make investments, or stay a while and open savings and checking accounts. If you want to count your pesos in Spanish, see Chapter 5 for a list of cardinal numbers.

Get Me to the Bank

No matter why you need to visit a bank, the mini-dictionary in Table 6.1 will help you make your transaction smoothly.

Something Extra _____

In Spanish-speaking countries, banks are open from 9 A.M. to between 2 and 3 P.M. on weekdays and from 9 A.M. until 1 or 1:30 P.M. on Saturday. Most banks have departments for changing foreign currency and, oddly enough, tend to give better rates for traveler's checks than kiosks at the airports or hotels. It's important to bring along your passport. In banks, it's the only acceptable form of identification.

Una casa de cambio (oo-nah kah-sah day kahm-bee-yoh) also exchange money. These can be found all over the streets of Spanish-speaking countries. Some offer terrific rates; others charge exorbitant commissions. It's always a good idea to investigate a few before making a transaction.

Table 6.1   Mini-Dictionary of Banking Terms

Term	Spanish	Pronunciation
advance payment	el pago adelantado	ehl pah-goh ah-deh-lahn-tah-doh

Term	Spanish	Pronunciation
automatic teller machine	el cajero automático	ehl kah-heh-roh ow-toh-mah-tee-koh
balance	el saldo	ehl sahl-doh
bank	el banco	ehl bahn-koh
bank account	la cuenta bancaria	lah kweh-tah bahn-kah-ree-yah
bankbook	la cartilla de ahorros	lah kahr-tee-yah deh ah-oh-rrohs
	la libreta de ahorros	lah lee-breh-tah deh ah-oh-rrohs
bank note	el billete de banco	ehl bee-yeh-teh deh bahnn-koh
bill	la factura	lah fahk-too-rah
to borrow	prestar	prehs-tahr
branch	la sucursal	lah soo-koor-sahl
cash	el dinero en efectivo	ehl dee-neh-roh ehn eh-fehk-tee-boh
to cash	cobrar	koh-brahr
cash flow	la corriente en efectivo	lah koh-rree-yeh-teh ehn eh-fehk-tee-boh
	los movimientos en efectivos	lohs moh-bee-mee-yehn-tohs ehn eh-fehk-tee-bohs
	el flujo de efectivo	ehl floo-hoh deh eh-fehk-tee-boh
cashier	el cajero	ehl kah-heh-roh
change (transaction)	el cambio	ehl kahm-bee-yoh
change (coins)	la moneda	lah moh-neh-dah
check	el cheque	ehl cheh-keh

continues

Table 6.1 Mini-Dictionary of Banking Terms
(continued)

Term	Spanish	Pronunciation
checkbook	la chequera	lah cheh-keh-rah
checking account	la cuenta corriente	lah kwehn-tah koh-rree-yen-teh
coin	la moneda	lah moh-neh-dah
credit	el crédito	ehl kreh-dee-toh
currency (foreign)	el dinero (la divisa)	ehl dee-neh-roh (lah dee-bee-sah)
customer	el cliente	ehl klee-yehn-teh
debt	la deuda	lah deh-oo-dah
deposit	el depósito el ingreso	ehl deh-poh-see-toh ehl een-greh-soh
to deposit	depositar ingresar	deh-poh-see-tahr een-greh-sahr
down payment	el desembolso inicial	ehl deh-sehm-bohl-soh ee-nee-see-yahl
due date	la fecha de vencimiento	lah feh-chah deh behn-see-mee-yehn-toh
employee	el empleado	ehl ehm-pleh-yah-doh
to endorse	endosar	ehn-doh-sahr
exchange rate	el tipo de cambio	ehl tee-poh deh kahm-bee-yoh
to fill out	llenar	yeh-nahr
final payment	el pago final	ehl pah-goh fee-nahl
guarantee	la garantía	lah gah-rahn-tee-yah
holder	el titular el portador el tenedor	ehl tee-too-lahr ehl pohr-tah-dohr ehl teh-neh-dohr

Term	Spanish	Pronunciation
installment payment	el pago (el abono) a plazos	ehl pah-goh (ehl ah-boh-noh) ah plah-sohs
installment plan	las facilidades de pago	lahs fah-see-lee-dah-dehs deh pah-goh
interest	el interés	ehl een-teh-rehs
simple	simple	seem-pleh
compound	compuesto	kohm-pwehs-toh
interest rate	la tasa (el tipo) de interés	lah tah-sah (ehl tee-poh) deh een-teh-rehs
to invest	invertir	een-behr-teer
investment	la inversión	lah een-behr-see-yohn
loan	el préstamo	ehl prehs-tah-moh
to take out a loan	hacer un préstamo	ah-sehr oon prehs-tah-moh
long term	a largo plazo	ah lahr-goh plah-soh
to manage	administrar manejar	ahd-mee-nees-trahr mah-neh-hahr
money exchange bureau	el departamento de intercambio	ehl deh-pahr-tah-mehn-toh deh een-tehr-kahm-bee-yoh
monthly statement	el extracto de cuenta el estado de cuenta el mensual	ehl ehks-trahk-toh deh kwehn-tah ehl ehs-tah-doh deh kwehn-tah, ehl men-soo-wahl
mortgage	la hipoteca	lah ee-poh-teh-kah

continues

Table 6.1   Mini-Dictionary of Banking Terms
(continued)

Term	Spanish	Pronunciation
open account	la cuenta corriente	lah kwehn-tah koh-rree-yehn-teh
overdrawn check	el cheque sin fondos	ehl cheh-keh seen fohn-dohs
overdraft	el giro en descubierto	ehl hee-roh ehn dehs-koo-bee-yehr-toh
	el saldo deudor	ehl sahl-doh deh-oo-dohr
to pay cash	pagar en efectivo	pah-gahr ehn eh-fehk-tee-boh
payment	el pago	ehl pah-goh
percent	por ciento	pohr see-yehn-toh
percentage	el porcentaje	ehl pohr-sehn-tah-heh
PIN number	el número de identificación personal	ehl noo-meh-roh deh ee-dehn-tee-fee-kah-see-yohn pehr-soh-nahl
promissory note	el pagaré	ehl pah-gah-reh
to purchase	comprar	kohm-prahr
to put	poner	poh-nehr
quarter	el trimestre	ehl tree-mehs-treh
receipt	el recibo	ehl reh-see-boh
revenue	los ingresos	lohs een-greh-sohs
safe	la caja fuerte	lah kah-hah fwehr-teh
sale	la venta	lah behn-tah
to save	ahorrar	ah-oh-rrahr

Term	Spanish	Pronunciation
savings account	la cuenta de ahorros	lah kwehn-tah deh ah-oh-rrohs
short term	a corto plazo	ah kohr-toh plah-soh
to sign (to)	firmar	feer-mahr
signature	la firma	lah feer-mah
sum	el monto el total	ehl mohn-toh ehl toh-tahl
teller	la suma el cajero	lah soo-mah ehl kah-heh-roh
total	el total el monto	ehl toh-tahl ehl mohn-toh
transfer	la transferencia	lah trahs-feh-rehn-see-yah
traveler's check	el cheque de viajero	ehl cheh-keh deh bee-yah-heh-roh
void (to void)	inválido (anular)	een-bah-lee-doh (ah-noo-lahr)
window	la ventanilla	lah behn-tah-nee-yah
to withdraw	sacar retirar	sah-kahr rreh-tee-rahr
withdrawal	la retirada	lah rreh-tee-rah-dah

Banking Transactions

The following phrases will be most helpful in common, everyday banking situations such as making deposits and withdrawals, opening a checking account, or taking out a loan.

What are the banking hours?
¿Cuáles son las horas de abertura y de cierre?
kwah-lehs sohn lahs oh-rahs deh ah-behr-too-rah ee deh see-yeh-reh

I would like …
Quisiera …
kee-see-yeh-rah

> to make a deposit.
> *hacer un depósito.*
> ah-sehr oon deh-poh-see-toh

> to make a withdrawal.
> *hacer un retiro.*
> ah-sehr oon reh-tee-roh

> to make a payment.
> *hacer un pago.*
> ah-sehr oon pah-goh

> to apply for a loan.
> *pedir un préstamo.*
> peh-deer oon prehs-tah-moh

> to cash a check.
> *cobrar un cheque.*
> koh-brahr oon cheh-keh

> to open an account.
> *abrir una cuenta.*
> ah-breer oo-nah kwehn-tah

> to close an account.
> *liquidar una cuenta.*
> lee-kee-dahr oo-nah kwehn-tah

> to change some foreign money.
> *cambiar divisas.*
> kahm-bee-yahr dee-bee-sahs

Will I get a monthly statement?
¿Recibiré un extracto de cuentas (un estado de cuenta) mensual?
rreh-see-bee-reh oon ehks-trahk-toh deh kwehn-tahs (oon ehs-tah-doh deh kwehn-tah) meh-soo-wahl

What is the status of my account?
¿Cuál es el estado de mi cuenta?
kwahl ehs ehl ehs-tah-doh deh mee kwehn-tah

What net yearly rate will I receive?
¿Qué anualidad neta de impuestos recibiré?
keh ah-noo-wah-lee-dahd neh-tah deh eem-pwehs-tohs rreh-see-bee-reh

What is today's exchange rate?
¿Cuál es la tasa (el tipo) de cambio hoy del dólar?
kwahl ehs lah tah-sah (ehl tee-poh) deh kahm-bee-yoh oy dehl doh-lahr

I would like the money in (large) bills (in small change).
Quisiera el dinero en billetes (grandes) (en suelto).
kee-see-yeh-rah ehl dee-neh-roh ehn bee-yeh-tehs (grahn-dehs) (ehn swehl-toh)

Is there a financial assistant who can help me?
¿Hay un(a) especialista financiero(a) que pueda ayudarme (aconsejarme)?
ahy oon (oo-nah) ehs-peh-see-yah-lees-tah fee-nahn-see-yeh-roh(ah) keh pweh-dah ah-yoo-dahr-meh (ah-kohn-seh-hahr-meh)

Do you have an automatic teller machine?
¿Tiene Ud. un cajero automático?
tee-yeh-neh oo-stehd oon kah-heh-roh ow-toh-mah-tee-koh

How does one use it?
¿Cómo se usa?
koh-moh seh oo-sah

Is it available all the time?
¿Es disponible todo el tiempo?
ehs dees-poh-nee-bleh toh-doh ehl tee-yehm-poh

Can I take my money out 24 hours a day?
¿Puedo retirar (sacar) mi dinero veinte y cuatro horas al día?
pweh-doh reh-tee-rahr (sah-kahr) mee dee-neh-roh behn-teh ee kwah-troh oh-rahs ahl día

Is there a commission fee for each transaction?
¿Hay una comisión para cada transacción?
ahy oo-nah koh-mee-see-yohn pah-rah kah-dah trahns-ahk-see-yohn

I'd like to apply for a mortgage.
Quisiera pedir una hipoteca.
kee-see-yeh-rah peh-deer oo-nah ee-poh-teh-kah

What is the time period of the loan?
¿Cuál es el plazo del préstamo?
kwahl ehs ehl plah-soh dehl prehs-tah-moh

How much are the monthly payments?
¿A cuántas son las mensualidades?
ah kwahn-tohs sohn lahs mehn-soo-wah-lee-dah-dehs

What is the interest rate?
¿Cuál es la tasa (el tipo) de interés?
kwahl ehs lah tah-sah (ehl tee-poh) deh
een-teh-rehs

Is it a fixed or variable rate?
Es una tasa (un tipo) fija (fijo) o variable?
ehs oo-nah tah-sah (oon tee-poh) fee-hah
(fee-hoh) oh bah-ree-yah-bleh

What are the terms of payment?
¿Cuáles son las condiciones de pago?
kwah-lehs sohn lahs kohn-dee-see-yoh-nehs
deh pah-goh

What are the methods of payment?
¿Cuáles son los métodos de pago?
kwah-lehs sohn lohs meh-toh-dohs deh pah-goh

Is the mortgage transferable?
¿Es transferible la hipoteca?
ehs trahns-feh-ree-bleh lah ee-poh-teh-kah

When is it necessary to start making payments?
¿Cuándo tengo que empezar a hacer pagos?
kwahn-doh tehn-goh keh ehm-peh-sahr ah ah-
sehr pah-gohs

Money and More Money

As in many European countries, the euro is the cur-
rency of Spain. In Mexico, it's the Mexican peso.
The following currencies are currently used in
Spanish-American countries:

Country	Currency	Pronunciation
Argentina	peso	peh-soh
Bolivia	boliviano	boh-lee-bee-yah-noh
Chile	chileno	chee-leh-noh
Colombia	peso	peh-soh
Costa Rica	colón	koh-lohn
Cuba	peso	peh-soh
Dominican Republic	peso	peh-soh
Ecuador	sucre	soo-kreh
El Salvador	colón	koh-lohn
Guatemala	quetzal	keht-sahl
Honduras	lempira	lehm-pee-rah
Mexico	nuevo peso	nweh-boh peh-soh
Nicaragua	nueva córdoba	nweh-bah kohr-doh-bah
Panama	balboa	bahl-boh-ah
Peru	nuevo sol	nweh-boh sohl
Puerto Rico	dólar estado-unidense	doh-lahr ehs-tah-doh-oo-nee-dehn-seh
Spain	euro	oo-roh
Uruguay	nuevo peso	nweh-boh peh-soh
Venezuela	bolívar	boh-lee-bahr

Hotel Hospitality

In This Chapter

- Deciding where to stay
- Hotel amenities
- Ordinal Numbers

No matter where you go in the Spanish-speaking world, a U.S. travel agent can help you find accommodations and make reservations that suit both your needs and your budget. For the more adventurous traveler, it might prove more economical to bargain for a room rate in Mexico or in rural areas throughout the Spanish-speaking world.

Hotel Accommodations

If you plan to stay in a Spanish-speaking country, possible accommodations include the following:

- *Un hotel* (oon oh-tehl) is usually rated by the government or a travel-rating organization using a star system ranging from inexpensive (one star) to very expensive (five stars).

Every hotel has an outside plaque indicating an *H* for hotel.

- *Una pensión* (oo-nah pehn-see-yohn) is similar to a rooming house, where guests pay for a room and all or part of their meals.

- *Un albergue* (oon ahl-behr-geh) is a small, modest inn generally found in rural areas. *Los albergues juveniles* (lohs ahl-behr-gwehs hoo-beh-nee-lehs) are youth hostels.

- *Un parador* (oon pah-rah-dohr) offers the most luxurious hotel accommodations. Some former royal homes, converted castles and palaces, or monasteries are run as *paradores*.

- *Un hostal* (oon ohs-tahl) is a small hotel or inn without a restaurant.

- *Un refugio* (oon rreh-foo-hee-yoh) is a private retreat or lodge in the country that may be rented for a specified time period.

What a Place! Does It Have ... ?

Before leaving home, you probably should check with your travel agent or the hotel's management to make sure the hotel you've chosen has the amenities you desire. Depending on your requirements, you need to know the words for everything from "bathroom" to "swimming pool." See Table 7.1 for a basic list of hotel amenities.

Is (Are) there ...?
¿Hay ...? (pronounced ahy)

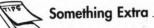

Something Extra _____

In Spanish buildings, the ground floor is called *la planta baja* (lah plahn-tah bah-hah), which literally means "the lower floor." The basement is called *el sótano* (ehl soh-tah-noh). Expect to see the abbreviations PB and Sót. for these levels on elevator buttons. The word *piso* (pee-soh) refers to floors above ground level.

Table 7.1   Hotel Facilities

Term	Spanish	Pronunciation
a bar	un bar	oon bahr
a bellman	un portero	oon pohr-teh-roh
a business center	un centro de negocios	oon sehn-troh deh neh-goh-see-yohs
a concierge	un conserje	oon koh-sehr-heh
a doorman	un portero	oon pohr-teh-roh
an elevator	un ascensor	oon ah-sehn-sohr
a fitness center	un gimnasio	oon heem-nah-see-yoh
a gift shop	una tienda de regalos	oo-nah tee-yehn-dah deh rreh-gah-lohs
a laundry and dry cleaning service	una lavandería	oo-nah lah-bahn-deh-ree-yah
maid service	una gobernanta	oo-nah goh-behr-nahn-tah
a restaurant	un restaurante	oon rrehs-tow-rahn-teh

continues

Table 7.1 Hotel Facilities (continued)

Term	Spanish	Pronunciation
a swimming pool	una piscina	oo-nah pee-see-nah
valet parking	una atendencia del garaje	oo-nah ah-tehn-dehn-see-yah dehl gah-rah-heh

Checking In to Your Hotel

When you check in, you may want to use the following phrases:

> I'd like a double (single) room, please.
> *Quisiera una habitación con dos camas (una sola cama) por favor.*
> kee-see-yeh-rah oo-nah ah-bee-tah-see-yohn kohn dohs kah-mahs (oo-nah soh-lah kah-mah) pohr fah-bohr
>
> I don't have a reservation.
> *No tengo reserva.*
> noh tehn-goh rreh-sehr-bah
>
> May I see the room?
> *¿Puedo ver la habitación?*
> poo-weh-doh behr lah ah-bee-tah-see-yohn
>
> I (don't) like it.
> *(No) Me gusta.*
> (noh) meh goos-tah

Could you put another bed in the room?
¿Podría poner otra cama en la habitación?
poo-dree-yah poh-nehr oh-trah kah-mah ehn
lah ah-bee-tah-see-yohn

How much is the room?
¿Cuánto cuesta la habitación?
kwahn-toh kwehs-tah lah ah-bee-tah-see-yohn

> with breakfast
> *con desayuno*
> kohn deh-sah-yoo-noh

> without meals
> *sin comidas*
> seen koh-mee-dahs

How much extra do we have to pay?
¿Cuánto más tenemos que pagar?
kwahn-toh mahs teh-neh-mohs keh pah-gahr

May I please have the key?
¿Puedo obtener la llave, por favor?
pweh-doh ohb-teh-nehr lah yah-beh pohr fah-
bohr

Getting What You Want

If you need something to make your stay more enjoyable, don't be afraid to speak up. Table 7.2 lists a
few items you might want or need.

I would like …	Please send me …
Quisiera …	*Haga el favor de mandarme …*
kee-see-yeh-rah	hah-gah ehl fah-bohr deh mahn-dahr-meh

I need ...   There isn't (aren't) ...
Me falta(n) ...   *No hay ...*
meh fahl-tah(n)   noh ahy

I need ...
Necesito ...
neh-seh-see-toh

Table 7.2   Wants and Needs

Phrase	Spanish	Pronunciation
air conditioning	aire acondicionado	ahy-reh ah-kohn-dee-syoh-nah-doh
an alarm clock	un despertador	oon dehs-pehr-tah-dohr
an ashtray	un cenicero	oon seh-nee-seh-roh
a balcony	un balcón	oon bahl-kohn
a bar of soap	una pastilla de jabón	oo-nah pahs-tee-yah deh hah-bohn
a bellhop	un botones	oon boh-toh-nehs
a blanket	una manta	oo-nah mahn-tah
a chambermaid	una camarera	oo-nah kah-mah-reh-rah
a hair dryer	un secador de pelo	oon seh-kah-dohr deh peh-loh
hangers	unas perchas	oo-nahs pehr-chahs
ice cubes	cubitos de hielo	hoo-bee-tohs deh yeh-loh
a key	una llave	oo-nah yah-beh
mineral water rahl	agua mineral	ah-gwah mee-neh-
on the courtyard	con vista al patio	kohn bees-tah ahl pah-tee-yoh

Phrase	Spanish	Pronunciation
on the garden	con vista al jardín	kohn bees-tah ahl har-deen
on the sea	con vista al mar	kohn bees-tah ahl mahr
a pillow	una almohada	oo-nah ahl-moh-ah-dah
a roll of toilet paper	un rollo de papel higiénico	oon rroh-yoh deh pah-pehl ee-hee-yeh-nee-koh
a room	una habitación	oo-nah ah-bee-tah-see-yohn
a safe (deposit box)	una caja de seguridad	oo-nah kah-hah deh seh-goo-ree-dahd
a telephone	un teléfono	oon teh-leh-foh-noh
a television (color)	una televisión (en color)	oo-nah teh-leh-bee-see-yohn (ehn koh-lohr)
tissues	pañuelos de papel	pah-nyoo-weh-lohs deh pah-pehl
a towel	una toalla	oo-nah toh-wah-yah
a transformer (an adaptor)	un transform-ador	oon trahns-fohr-mah-dohr

Bathroom Etiquette

In many foreign countries, especially in older establishments, the sink and bathtub (and/or shower) are
located in what is called the bathroom—*el baño*
(ehl bah-nyoh)—whereas the toilet and bidet are in
the water closet—*el W.C.* (ehl doh-bleh-beh seh).

Showers are often of the handheld type and are not affixed to the wall, which sometimes makes them rather difficult to negotiate.

Something Extra

A bidet is a marvelous accessory that can be found in many foreign countries. It allows a person to clean his or her private parts in a very discreet way. The user must face forward, straddle the bidet, and manually turn on controlled jets of hot and cold water. It is not for feet or dirty laundry.

When There's a Problem

Upon arrival, it is not uncommon to find that your room isn't exactly what you expected. Use the following phrases when you have a problem:

I don't like the room.
No me gusta la habitación.
noh meh goos-tah lah ah-bee-tah-see-yohn

Do you have something …?
¿Hay algo …?
ahy ahl-goh

better	*mejor*	meh-hohr
cheaper	*más barato*	mahs bah-rah-toh
bigger	*más grande*	mahs grahn-deh
quieter	*más privado*	mahs pree-bah-doh
smaller	*más pequeño*	mahs peh-keh-nyoh

The lamp doesn't work.
La lámpara no funciona.
lah lahm-pah-rah noh foonk-see-yoh-nah

Can you fix it as soon as possible?
¿Puede arreglarlo(la) lo más pronto posible?
pweh-deh ah-rreh-glahr-loh(lah) loh mahs
prohn-toh poh-see-bleh

Up, Up, and Away

We've all had an elevator experience—either in a
hotel or elsewhere—in which we've felt like a large
sardine in a small can. When you're pushed to the
back or squished to the side, you have to hope that a
kind soul will ask, "*¿Qué piso, por favor?*" You will
need the ordinal numbers in Table 7.3 to give a correct answer, such as "*El segundo piso, por favor.*"

Table 7.3   Ordinal Numbers

No.	Spanish	Pronun-ciation	No.	Spanish	Pronun-ciation
1st	primero	pree-meh-roh	6th	sexto	sehks-toh
2nd	segundo	seh-goon-doh	7th	séptimo	sehp-tee-moh
3rd	tercero	tehr-seh-roh	8th	octavo	ohk-tah-boh
4th	cuarto	kwahr-toh	9th	noveno	noh-beh-noh
5th	quinto	keen-toh	10th	décimo	deh-see-moh

When using ordinal numbers, keep the following in mind:

- Change the final -*o* of the masculine form to -*a* to make ordinal numbers feminine.

el segundo acto	the second act
la segunda escena	the second scene

- In Spanish, only use ordinal numbers through the tenth. After that, cardinal numbers are used.

la Tercera Avenida	Third Avenue
la página treinta	page 30

- The words *primero* and *tercero* drop their final -*o* before a masculine, singular noun.

el primer hombre	the first man
la primera mujer	the first woman
el tercer día	the third day
la tercera semana	the third week

But

el siglo tercero	the third century

¡Cuidado!

When a cardinal number is used as an ordinal number, it is always masculine.

la página doscientos
page 200

Chapter 8

What a Gorgeous Day!

In This Chapter

- The weather
- Days of the week
- Months of the year
- Seasons
- Remembering a date

Whenever you plan a trip, you need to know what weather to anticipate so you can plan and pack properly. Remember that in South American countries below the equator, the seasons are the opposite of what we experience here. And after you arrive in a country, you'll want to be able to read or listen to the weather forecast (*el pronóstico*, ehl proh-nohs-tee-koh) so you can arrange your sightseeing trips and outings accordingly.

What's the Weather?

The phrases in Table 8.1 will help you with the weather.

Table 8.1 Weather Expressions

Expression	Spanish	Pronunciation
What's the weather?	¿Qué tiempo hace?	keh tee-yehm-poh ah-seh
It's beautiful.	Hace buen tiempo.	ah-seh bwehn tee-yehm-poh
It's hot.	Hace calor.	ah-seh kah-lohr
It's sunny.	Hace sol.	ah-seh sohl
It's nasty (bad).	Hace mal tiempo.	ah-seh mahl tee-yehm-poh
It's cold.	Hace frío.	ah-seh free-yoh
It's cool.	Hace fresco.	ah-seh frehs-koh
It's windy.	Hace viento.	ah-seh bee-yehn-toh
It's lightning.	Hay relámpagos.	ahy rreh-lahm-pah-gohs
It's thundering.	Truena.	troo-weh-nah
It's foggy.	Hay niebla.	ahy nee-eh-blah
It's misty.	Hay neblina.	ahy neh-blee-nah
It's humid.	Hay humedad.	ahy oo-meh-dahd
It's cloudy.	Hay nubes. Está nublado.	ahy noo-behs ehs-tah noo-blah-doh
It's overcast.	Está cubierto.	ehs-tah koo-bee-yehr-toh
It's raining.	Llueve. Está lloviendo.	yoo-weh-beh ehs-tah yoh-bee-yehn-doh
It's pouring.	Hay lluvias torrenciales.	ahy yoo-bee-yahs toh-rrehn-see-yahl-ehs

Expression	Spanish	Pronunciation
It's snowing.	Nieva.	nee-eh-bah
	Está nevando.	ehs-tah neh-bahn-doh
There'a windstorm.	Hay un vendaval.	ahy oon behn-dah-vahl
There's hail.	Hay granizo.	ahy grah-nee-soh
There are showers.	Hay lluvias.	ahy yoo-bee-ahs

Baby, It's Hot Outside!

Expressing the temperature is different in Spanish-speaking countries. Why? They use the Centigrade (Celsius) scale rather than the Fahrenheit scale to which we are accustomed. This means that when the concierge tells you it's 20 degrees (Centigrade or Celsius), it's really a pleasant 68 degrees Fahrenheit. To convert Centigrade (Celsius) to Fahrenheit, multiply the Centigrade (Celsius) temperature by ⅘ (1.8) and then add 32. To ask for the temperature, simply say the following:

What's the temperature?
¿Cuál es la temperatura?
kwahl ehs lah tehm-peh-rah-too-rah

It's 50 degrees.
Hay una temperatura de cincuenta grados.
ahy oo-nah tehm-peh-rah-too-rah deh seen-kwehn-tah grah-dos

It's zero degrees.
Hay una temperatura de cero.
ahy oo-nah tehm-peh-rah-too-rah deh seh-roh

It's two degrees below zero.
Hay una temperatura de menos dos grados.
ahy oo-nah tehm-peh-rah-too-rah deh meh-nohs dohs grah-dos

What Day Is It?

Unlike our calendars, Spanish calendars start with Monday. Study the days of the week in Table 8.2 so you don't miss a thing.

In Spanish, only capitalize days of the week when they are at the beginning of a sentence. When used elsewhere, unlike in English, they are written with a lowercase first letter.

Sábado es un día.
Saturday is a day.

Voy al supermercado el sábado.
I go to the supermarket on Saturday.

Table 8.2   Days of the Week

Day	Spanish	Pronunciation
Monday	lunes	loo-nehs
Tuesday	martes	mahr-tehs
Wednesday	miércoles	mee-yehr-koh-lehs
Thursday	jueves	hoo-weh-behs

Day	Spanish	Pronunciation
Friday	viernes	bee-yehr-nehs
Saturday	sábado	sah-bah-doh
Sunday	domingo	doh-meen-goh

Something Extra

To express "on" when talking about a certain day, the Spanish use the definite article *el* or *los*.

Voy al cine el viernes.
I go to the movies on Friday.

No trabjo los domingos.
I don't work on Sundays.

My Favorite Month

As you glance through glossy vacation brochures, you want to be able to figure out the best time to take your trip. Table 8.3 gives you the names of the months so you don't wind up in the wrong place at the wrong time.

Table 8.3 Months of the Year

Month	Spanish	Pronunciation
January	enero	eh-neh-roh
February	febrero	feh-breh-roh
March	marzo	mahr-soh

continues

Table 8.3 Months of the Year (continued)

Month	Spanish	Pronunciation
April	abril	ah-breel
May	mayo	mah-yoh
June	junio	hoo-nee-yoh
July	julio	hoo-lee-yoh
August	agosto	ah-gohs-toh
September	septiembre	sehp-tee-yehm-breh
October	octubre	ohk-too-breh
November	noviembre	noh-bee-yehm-breh
December	diciembre	dee-see-yehm-breh

Unless used at the beginning of a sentence, the names of all months should be written all lowercase.

> *Enero es un mes.*
> January is a month.
> *Voy a España en enero.*
> I go to Spain in January.

To Every Season Turn, Turn, Turn

Make sure to plan your trip for when the weather will be great so you don't have to worry about hurricanes, storms, or other adverse conditions. Table 8.4 provides the names of the seasons.

Table 8.4   The Seasons

Season	Spanish	Pronunciation
winter	el invierno	ehl een-bee-yehr-noh
spring	la primavera	lah pree-mah-beh-rah
summer	el verano	ehl beh-rah-noh
autumn, fall	el otoño	ehl oh-toh-nyoh

When's Our Date?

No doubt, when making travel plans and arrange-
ments, you often will have to refer to and ask for
dates. Ask the following questions when you need
information about the day and the date:

> What day is it (today)?
> *¿Qué día es (hoy)?*
> keh dee-yah ehs (oy)

> What is (today's) the date?
> *¿Cuál es la fecha (de hoy)?*
> kwahl ehs lah feh-chah (deh oy)

The Spanish use the preposition *en* + the definite article for all seasons to express "in." Here's how it's done:

> *Voy a México en el invierno.*
> I go to Mexico in the winter.

You need to know how to express the date for appoint-
ments, travel plans, and meetings. In Spanish-
speaking countries, the date is expressed as follows:

day of week + *el* + (cardinal) number + *de* + month + *de* + year

Hoy es sábado el nueve de mayo de dos mil tres.
Estamos a sábado el nueve de mayo de dos mil tres.
Today is Saturday, May 9, 2003.

Use *primero* to express the first of each month.

el primero de mayo
May 1

But

el veintiuno de mayo
May 21

Do not use hundreds, as we do in English, when giving the year.

mil novecientos noventa y nueve 1999

Use the definite article to express "on" with dates.

Me voy el once de julio.
I'm leaving on July 11.

 ¡Cuidado! _____

Notice how the date is written in Spanish:

el 14 de septiembre de 1947 (14.9.47)
September 14, 1947 (9/14/47)

Chapter 9

Painting the Town Red

In This Chapter

- Sights for tourists
- How to make suggestions and plans
- How to give your opinion

When you travel to a foreign country, make sure to plan a logical itinerary of interesting sights to see.

Seeing the Sights

Whether you decide to go it alone or opt to take a tour, the following phrases will come in handy:

Where is there a tourist office?
¿Dónde hay una oficina de turismo?
dohn-deh ahy oo-nah oh-fee-see-nah deh too-rees-moh

What is there to see?
¿Qué hay para ver?
keh ahy pah-rah behr

Where can I buy a map (a guidebook)?
¿Dónde puedo comprar un mapa (una guía)?
dohn-deh pweh-doh kohm-prahr oon mah-pah
(oo-nah gee-yah)

At what time does it open (close)?
¿A qué hora se abre (se cierra)?
ah keh oh-rah seh ah-breh (seh see-yeh-rah)

What's the admission price?
¿Cuánto es la entrada?
kwahn-toh ehs lah ehn-trah-dah

Can children enter for free?
¿Pueden entrar gratis los niños?
pweh-dehn ehn-trahr grah-tees lohs nee-nyohs

Until what age?
¿Hasta qué edad?
ahs-tah keh eh-dahd

How much do they pay?
¿Cuánto pagan?
kwahn-toh pah-gahn

Is it all right to take pictures?
¿Se puede sacar fotos?
seh pweh-deh sah-kahr foh-tohs

I need a guide who speaks English.
Necesito un guía que hable inglés.
neh-seh-see-toh oon gee-yah keh ah-bleh
een-glehs

How much does he (she) charge?
¿Cuánto cobra?
kwahn-toh koh-brah

May I Suggest ...?

You've always had your heart set on seeing a bull-fight. You don't know, however, how the others in your group feel about accompanying you. Go for it! Make the suggestion. There are several easy ways to do this.

Try asking this simple question:

> *¿Por qué no + nosotros* form of the verb?
> Why don't we ...?
>
> *¿Por qué no vamos al cine?*
> pohr keh noh bah-mohs ahl see-neh
> Why don't we go to the movies?

Try telling a friend what you'd like to do and then ask for his or her feelings about the idea.

> *Quiero ir al cine. ¿Qué crees (piensas)?*
> kee-yeh-roh eer ahl see-neh
> keh kreh-yehs (pee-yehn-sahs)
> I want to go to the movies. What do you think?

Want to say "let's?" Use *vamos a* + the infinitive of the verb suggesting the activity.

> *Vamos a ver una corrida de toros.*
> bah-mohs ah behr oo-nah koh-rree-dah deh
> toh-rohs
> Let's see a bullfight.

Colloquially Speaking

If you're feeling rather confident with the language at this point, you might want to take a more colloquial approach to expressing yourself. You can use a number of phrases, all of which are followed by the infinitive of the verb. (The familiar *tú* forms are in parentheses.)

Phrase	Pronunciation	Meaning
¿Le (te) parece ...?	leh (teh) pah-reh-seh	Do you want ...?
¿Le (te) gustaría ...?	leh (teh) goos-tah-ree-yah	Would you like ...?
¿Tiene(s) ganas de ...?	tee-yeh-neh(s) gah-hans deh	Do you feel like ...?
¿Quiere(s) ...?	kee-yeh-reh(s)	Do you want ...?

> *¿Le (te) gustaría ir al museo?*
> Would you like to go to the museum?
>
> *¿Tiene(s) ganas de ver una corrida de toros?*
> Do you feel like seeing a bullfight?

Only petulant teenagers give abrupt yes or no answers to questions. Most of the rest of us say "Yes, but ..." or "No, because ..." If you'd like to elaborate on your answer, change the pronoun *le* or *te* from the question to *me* in your answer, as follows:

> *Sí, me parece ir al museo.*
> *No, no me gustaría ir al museo.*

So What Do You Think?

How do you feel about a suggestion made to you?
Does the activity appeal to you? If so, you would
say the following:

Phrase	Spanish	Pronunciation
I like ...	Me gusta ...	meh goos-tah
I adore ...	Me encanta ...	meh ehn-kahn-tah
I'm a fan of ...	Soy aficionado(a) de ...	soy ah-fee-see-yoh-nah-doh(dah) deh

> *Me gusta el arte.*
> meh goos-tah ehl ahr-teh
> I like art.
>
> *Me encanta la música.*
> meh ehn-kahn-tah lah moo-see-kah
> I adore music.
>
> *Soy aficionado(a) a la ópera.*
> soy ah-fee-see-yoh-nah-doh(dah) ah lah
> oh-peh-rah
> I'm an opera fan.

When you do something or go somewhere new, different, exotic, or out of the ordinary, you're bound
to have an opinion about whether you like it. Is it
fun? Are you having a good time? Are you amused?
Give your positive opinion by using *es* (ehs, meaning "it is") + an adjective.

Adjective	Spanish	Pronunciation
awesome	bárbaro	bahr-bah-roh
excellent	excelente	ehk-seh-leh-teh
extraordinary	extraordinario	ehs-trah-ohr-dee-nah-ree-yoh
fabulous	fabuloso	fah-boo-loh-soh
fantastic	fantástico	fahn-tahs-tee-koh
fun	divertido	dee-behr-tee-doh
great	regio	rreh-hee-yoh
magnificent	magnífico	mag-nee-fee-koh
marvelous	maravilloso	mah-rah-bee-yoh-soh
out of this world	de película	deh peh-lee-koo-lah
phenomenal	fenomenal	feh-noh-meh-nahl
sensational	sensacional	sehn-sah-see-yoh-nahl
stupendous	estupendo	ehs-too-pehn-doh
terrific	terrífico	teh-rree-fee-koh

Something Extra

When referring to just one thing, use *me gusta* and *me encanta*. When referring to more than one, use *me gustan* and *me encantan*.

> *Me gusta el museo.*
> *Me gustan los museos.*

Perhaps you don't like the suggestion presented. Maybe the activity bores you. To express your dislike, you might say the following:

Phrase	Spanish	Pronunciation
I don't like ...	No me gusta ...	noh meh goos-tah
I hate ...	Odio, Detesto ...	oh-dee-yoh, deh-tehs-toh
I'm not a fan of ...	No soy aficionado(a) de ...	noh soy ah-fee-see-yoh-nah-doh(dah) deh

To be a good sport, you tried the activity anyway. It was just as you thought—not your cup of tea. To give your negative opinion about an activity, you can use *es* (ehs, meaning "it is") + an adjective.

Adjective	Spanish	Pronunciation
boring	aburrido	ah-boo-rree-doh
disagreeable	desagradable	deh-sah-grah-dah-bleh
a disaster	un desastre	oon deh-sahs-treh
horrible	horrible	oh-rree-bleh
a horror	un horror	oon oh-rrohr
loathsome	asqueroso	ahs-keh-roh-soh
ridiculous	ridículo	rree-dee-koo-loh
silly	tonto	tohn-toh
terrible	terrible	teh-rree-bleh
ugly	feo	feh-yoh

Shopping Around

In This Chapter

- Stores
- Clothing, colors, sizes, materials, and designs
- Expressing your opinion

Perhaps you are very particular about what you purchase in the way of a gift or clothing, especially when you're in a foreign country. Of course you want to pick out the perfect memento or gift. You'll need to know how to express the color, size, material, and design of any article of clothing. You'll undoubtedly want to find bargains and do some comparison shopping. No matter what your plan of action, shopping can be made a pleasant and enjoyable experience for everyone.

Shopping 'til You Drop

Do you prefer to browse in chic boutiques? Do you like to bargain in outdoor markets? Or are you attracted by a large, elegant mall (*un centro comercial,* oon sehn-troh koh-mehr-see-yahl)? The following list points you in the direction of stores (*las tiendas,* lahs tee-yehn-dahs) that might interest you:

bookstore
la líbrería
lah lee-breh-ree-yah

newsstand
el quiosco de periódicos
ehl kee-yohs-koh deh peh-ree-yoh-dee-kohs

clothing store
la tienda de ropa
lah tee-yehn-dah deh rroh-pah

record store
la tienda de discos
lah tee-yehn-dah deh dees-kohs

department store
el almacén
ehl ahl-mah-sehn

souvenir shop
la tienda de recuerdos
lah tee-yehn-dah deh rreh-kwehr-dohs

florist
la florería
lah floh-reh-ree-yah

tobacco store
la tabaquería
lah tah-bah-keh-ree-yah

jewelry store
la joyería
lah hoh-yeh-ree-yah

toy store
la juguetería
lah hoo-geh-teh-ree-yah

leather goods store
la marroquinería
lah mah-rroh-kee-neh-ree-yah

If you are buying jewelry, you might want to ask the following questions:

¿Es macizo?
ehs mah-see-soh
Is it solid gold?

¿Es dorado?
ehs doh-rah-doh
Is it gold plated?

¿Es platino?
ehs plah-tee-noh
Is it platinum?

¿Es plata?
ehs plah-tah
Is it silver?

General Shopping Questions

Where can I find ...?
¿Dónde se puede encontrar ...?
dohn-deh seh pweh-deh ehn-kohn-trahr

Could you please help me?
¿Podría ayudarme, por favor?
poh-dree-yah ah-yoo-dahr-meh pohr fah-bohr

Would you please show me ...?
¿Pudiera enseñarme ..., por favor?
poo-dee-yeh-rah ehn-seh-nyahr-meh pohr
fah-bohr

Are there any sales?
¿Hay ventas (gangas)?
ahy behn-tahs (gahn-gahs)

Are there any discounts?
¿Hay rebajas (descuentos)?
ahy rreh-bah-hahs (dehs-kwehn-tohs)

Do you sell ...?
¿Se vende ...?
seh behn-deh

Where is (are) …?
¿Dónde está(n) …?
dohn-deh ehs-tah(n)

Do you have something …?
¿Tiene algo …?
tee-yeh-neh ahl-goh

Adjective	Spanish	Pronunciation
else	más	mahs
larger	más grande	mahs grahn-deh
smaller	más pequeño	mahs peh-keh-nyoh
longer	más largo	mahs lahr-goh
shorter	más corto	mahs kohr-toh
less expensive	más barato	mahs bah-rah-toh
more expensive	más caro	mahs kah-roh
better	de mejor	deh meh-hor

Does it come in another color?
¿Viene en otro color?
bee-yeh-neh ehn oh-troh koh-lohr

Can I try it on?
¿Puedo probármelo?
pweh-doh proh-bahr-meh-loh

Can you alter it?
¿Puede arreglarlo?
pweh-deh ah-rreh-glahr-loh

Can I return it?
¿Puedo devolverlo?
pweh-doh deh-bohl-behr-loh

Could you wrap it please?
¿Podría envolverlo, por favor?
poh-dree-yah ehn-bohl-behr-loh pohr fah-bohr

Do you take credit cards?
¿Acepta tarjetas de crédito?
ahk-sehp-tah tahr-heh-tahs deh kreh-dee-toh

Do you take traveler's checks?
¿Acepta cheques de viajero?
ah-sehp-tah cheh-kehs deh bee-yah-heh-roh

Clothing

It's always fun and interesting to buy an item of clothing (*la ropa*, lah rroh-pah) in a foreign country. The styles and patterns are really quite unique and often prove to be a topic of conversation. Whether you decide to be daring and buy something native or you crave something at the height of fashion (*a la última moda*, ah lah ool-tee-mah moh-dah), Table 10.1 will help you in your quest.

Table 10.1   Clothing

Clothing	Spanish	Pronunciation
For One and All		
bathing suit	el traje de baño	ehl trah-heh deh bah-nyoh
belt	el cinturón	ehl seen-too-rohn
boots	las botas	lahs boh-tahs

continues

Table 10.1 Clothing (continued)

Clothing	Spanish	Pronunciation
gloves	los guantes	lohs gwahn-tehs
hat	el sombrero	ehl sohm-breh-roh
jacket	la chaqueta	lah chah-keh-tah
jeans	los jeans	lohs jeens
overcoat	el abrigo	ehl ah-bree-goh
pants	los pantalones	lohs pahn-tah-loh-nehs
raincoat	el impermeable	ehl eem-pehr-meh-yah-bleh
robe	la bata	lah bah-tah
sandals	las sandalias	lahs sahn-dah-lee-yahs
scarf	la bufanda	lah boo-fahn-dah
shirt	la camisa	lah kah-mee-sah
shoes	los zapatos	lohs sah-pah-tohs
shorts	los pantalones cortos	lohs pahn-tah-loh-nehs kohr-tohs
sneakers	los tenis	lohs teh-nees
socks	los calcetines	lohs kahl-seh-tee-nehs
sweater	el suéter	ehl sweh-tehr
T-shirt	la camiseta, la playera	lah kah-mee-seh-tah, lah plah-yeh-rah
umbrella	el paraguas	ehl pah-rah-gwahs
underwear	la ropa interior	lah rroh-pah een-teh-ree-yohr

For Men Only

coat (sport)	el saco	ehl sah-koh
shorts (under garments)	los calzoncillos	lohs kahl-sohn-see-yohs
suit	el traje	ehl trah-heh

Clothing	Spanish	Pronunciation
tie	la corbata	lah kohr-bah-tah
undershirt	la camiseta	lah kah-mee-seh-tah

For Women Only

brassiere	el sostén	ehl sohs-tehn
blouse	la blusa	lah bloo-sah
dress	el vestido	ehl behs-tee-doh
negligee	el salto de cama	ehl sahl-toh deh kah-mah
panties	los pantaloncillos de mujer	lohs pahn-tah-lohn-see-yohs deh moo-hehr
pantyhose (tights)	las pantimedias	lahs pahn-tee-meh-dee-yahs
pocketbook	la bolsa	lah bohl-sah
skirt	la falda	lah fahl-dah
slip (half) (full)	el faldellín la combinación	ehl fahl-deh-yeen lah kohm-bee-nah-see-yohn
stockings	las medias	lahs meh-dee-yahs
suit	el traje sastre	ehl trah-heh sahs-treh

Of course, you want to make sure you wind up with items that fit. Tell the salesperson the following:

I wear size …	small	medium	large
Llevo el tamaño … yeh-boh ehl tah-mah-nyoh	*pequño* peh-keh-nyoh	*mediano* meh-dee-yah-noh	*grande* grahn-deh

Colors

Do you see the world in primary colors (*los colores,* lohs koh-loh-rehs)? Or do you tend to go for the more exotic, artistic shades? Table 10.2 will help you learn the basic colors so you can get by.

Table 10.2 Colors

Color	Spanish	Pronunciation
beige	beige	beh-heh
black	negro	neh-groh
blue	azul	ah-sool
brown	marrón, pardo	mah-rrohn, pahr-doh
gray	gris	grees
green	verde	behr-deh
orange	anaranjado	ah-nah-rahn-hah-doh
pink	rosado	rroh-sah-doh
purple	morado	moh-rah-doh
red	rojo	rroh-hoh
white	blanco	blahn-koh
yellow	amarillo	ah-mah-ree-yoh

Add the word *claro* (klah-roh) to describe a color as light. Add the word *oscuro* (oh-skoo-roh) to describe a color as dark.

light green | dark blue
verde claro | *azul oscuro*

Materials

Do you find linen sexy? Do you love the feel of silk? Do you crave the coolness of cotton? Is leather a turn-on? Are you into wrinkle-free? Table 10.3 will help you pick the materials (*las telas*, lahs teh-lahs) you prefer. Use the word *en* (ehn) when speaking about materials.

Table 10.3   Materials

Material	Spanish	Pronunciation
cashmere	casimir	kah-see-meer
cotton	algodón	ahl-goh-dohn
denim	tela tejana	teh-lah teh-hah-nah
flannel	franela	frah-neh-lah
lace	encaje	ehn-kah-heh
leather	cuero	kweh-roh
linen	lino	lee-noh
nylon	nilón	nee-lohn
satin	raso	rrah-soh
silk	seda	seh-dah
suede	gamuza	gah-moo-sah
wool	lana	lah-nah

Designs

Let's say you're on the hunt for a skirt like the ones worn by Spanish *señoritas*. Or maybe you'd like a pair of plaid golf pants because you really want to stand out. Or perhaps you're not even in the mood to shop, but you'd like to compliment someone on the good taste of his striped tie. Table 10.4 provides the words you need to describe patterns or designs (*los diseños*, lohs dee-seh-nyohs).

Table 10.4 Designs

Design	Spanish	Pronunciation
in a solid color	de color liso	deh koh-lohr lee-soh
with stripes	de rayas	deh rrah-yahs
with polka dots	de lunares	deh loo-nah-rehs
in plaid	de cuadros	deh kwah-drohs

Use a demonstrative adjective to express this, that, these, or those. Note that the adjective you choose depends upon the physical proximity of the noun to the speaker and listener.

Adjective	Masculine	Femimine
this (near speaker)	este (ehs-teh)	esta (ehs-tah)
these (near speaker)	estos (ehs-tohs)	estas (ehs-tahs)
that (near listener)	ese (eh-seh)	esa (eh-sah)
those (near listener)	esos (eh-sohs)	esas (eh-sahs)
that (far from speaker and listener)	aquel (ah-kehl)	aquella (ah-keh-yah)
those (far from speaker and listener)	aquellos (ah-keh-yohs)	aquellas (ah-keh-yahs)

Food, Glorious Food

In This Chapter

- Buying food
- How to express quantity
- How to order in a restaurant
- How to get the dish you want
- Special diets

Whether you stop by a local bodega or specialty store to grab a bite to tide you over or you make reservations in the fanciest of restaurants, you need to know how to ask for the foods you want and how to refuse those that don't have any appeal. You also want to make sure you order the proper quantity. This chapter will help you satisfy all your cravings.

Specialty Shops

Do you like to keep snacks in your hotel room, just in case you get the midnight munchies? Or have you rented a condo or an apartment and prefer to do your own cooking? In any Spanish-speaking country, you can enjoy the culinary delights that can be purchased in the shops listed in Table 11.1.

Table 11.1   Food Shops

grocery (vegetable) store	la abacería lah ah-bah-seh-ree-yah
butcher shop	la carnicería lah kahr-nee-seh-ree-yah
bakery	la panadería lah pah-nah-deh-ree-yah
delicatessen	la salchichonería lah sahl-chee-choh-neh-ree-yah
candy store	la confitería lah kohn-fee-teh-ree-yah
dairy store	la lechería lah leh-cheh-ree-yah
fruit store	la frutería lah froo-teh-ree-yah
pastry shop	la pastelería lah pahs-teh-leh-ree-yah
fish store	la pescadería lah pehs-kah-deh-ree-yah
supermarket	el supermercado ehl soo-pehr-mehr-kah-doh
liquor store	la tienda de licores lah tee-yehn-dah deh lee-koh-rehs

Many stores take their name from the product they sell, as follows:

pan (bread)	*panadería*
carne (meat)	*carnicería*
pastel (pie)	*pastelería*
leche (milk)	*lechería*
fruta (fruit)	*frutería*
pescado (fish)	*pescadería*

Food and More Food

Whether you're in a store or at a restaurant, knowing the Spanish names of the foods you like and dislike will put you at a distinct advantage. Use Tables 11.2 through 11.9 to pick and choose at will.

Table 11.2   Vegetables (Las Legumbres)

Vegetable	Spanish	Pronunciation
asparagus	los espárragos	lohs ehs-pah-rrah-gohs
beans (green)	las judías (Spain)	lahs hoo-dee-yahs
	los ejotes (Mexico)	lohs eh-hoh-tehs
	los porotos verdes (Chile)	lohs poh-roh-tohs behr-dehs
	las habichuelas (elsewhere)	lahs ah-bee-chweh-lahs
beet	la remolacha	lah rreh-moh-lah-chah
broccoli	el brócoli	ehl broh-koh-lee

continues

Table 11.2 Vegetables (Las Legumbres) (continued)

Vegetable	Spanish	Pronunciation
carrot	la zanahoria	lah sah-nah-hoh-ree-yah
cauliflower	la coliflor	lah koh-lee-flohr
celery	el apio	ehl ah-pee-yoh
chickpeas	los garbanzos	lohs gahr-bahn-sohs
corn	el maíz	ehl mah-yees
cucumber	el pepino	ehl peh-pee-noh
eggplant	la berenjena	lah beh-rehn-heh-nah
lettuce	la lechuga	lah leh-choo-gah
mushroom	el champiñon	ehl chahm-pee-nyohn
onion	la cebolla	lah seh-boh-lyah
peas	los guisantes	lohs gee-sahn-tehs
pepper	el pimiento	ehl pee-mee-yehn-toh
potato	la papa, la patata	lah pah-pah, lah pah-tah-tah
rice	el arroz	ehl ah-rohs
spinach	la espinaca	lah ehs-pee-nah-kah
squash	la cucurbitácea	lah koo-koor-bee-tah-seh-yah
sweet potato	la papa dulce	lah pah-pah dool-seh
tomato	el tomate	ehl toh-mah-teh
zucchini	el calabacín	ehl kah-lah-bah-seen

Table 11.3 Fruits (Las Frutas)

Fruit	Spanish	Pronunciation
apple	la manzana	lah mahn-sah-nah
apricot	el albaricoque	ehl ahl-bah-ree-koh-keh
banana (green)	la banana (el plátano)	lah bah-nah-nah (ehl plah-tah-noh)
blueberry	el mirtilo	ehl meer-tee-loh
cherry	la cereza	lah seh-reh-sah
coconut	el coco	ehl koh-koh
grape	la uva	lah oo-bah
grapefruit	el pomelo	ehl poh-meh-loh
lemon	el limón	ehl lee-mohn
lime	la lima	lah lee-mah
melon	el melón	ehl meh-lohn
olive	la aceituna	lah ah-seh-yee-too-nah
orange	la naranja	lah nah-rahn-hah
peach	el melocotón	ehl meh-loh-koh-tohn
pear	la pera	lah peh-rah
pineapple	la piña	lah pee-nyah
plum	la ciruela	lah see-roo-weh-lah
prune	la ciruela pasa	lah see-roo-weh-lah pah-sah
raisin	la uva seca	lah oo-bah seh-kah
raspberry	la frambuesa, la mora	lah frahm-bweh-sah, lah moh-rah
strawberry	la fresa	lah freh-sah
watermelon	la sandía	lah sahn-dee-yah

Table 11.4 Meats (Las Carnes)

Meat	Spanish	Pronunciation
beef	la carne de vaca	lah kahr-neh deh bah-kah
chop, cutlet	la chuleta	lah choo-leh-tah
chopped meat	la carne picada	lah kahr-neh pee-kah-dah
filet mignon	el lomo fino	ehl loh-moh fee-noh
ham	el jamón	ehl hah-mohn
hamburger	la hamburguesa	lah ahm-boor-geh-sah
lamb	la carne de cordero	lah kahr-neh deh kohr-deh-roh
liver	el hígado	ehl ee-gah-doh
pork	la carne de cerdo	lah kahr-neh deh sehr-doh
roast beef	el rosbíf	ehl rrohs-beef
sausage	el chorizo	ehl choh-ree-zoh
steak	el bistec	ehl bees-tehk
stew	el estofado, el guisado	ehl ehs-toh-fah-doh, ehl gee-sah-doh
veal	la carne de ternera	lah kahr-neh deh tehr-neh-rah

Table 11.5 Fowl and Game (La Carne de Ave y de Caza)

Fowl or Game	Spanish	Pronunciation
chicken	el pollo	ehl poh-yoh
duck	el pato	ehl pah-toh

Fowl or Game	Spanish	Pronunciation
rabbit	el conejo	ehl koh-neh-hoh
turkey	el pavo	ehl pah-boh

Table 11.6   Fish and Seafood (El Pescado y Los Mariscos)

Fish or Seafood	Spanish	Pronunciation
anchovy	la anchoa	la ahn-choh-ah
bass	la merluza	lah mehr-loo-sah
clam	la almeja	lah ahl-meh-hah
codfish	el bacalao	ehl bah-kah-lah-oh
crab	el cangrejo	ehl kahn-greh-hoh
flounder	el lenguado	ehl lehn-gwah-doh
grouper	el mero	ehl meh-roh
lobster	la langosta	lah lahn-gohs-tah
mackerel	la caballa	lah kah-bah-yah
monkfish	el rape	ehl rrah-peh
mussel	el mejillón	lah meh-hee-yohn
oyster	la ostra	lah ohs-trah
red snapper	el pargo colorado	ehl pahr-goh koh-loh-rah-doh
scallops	las conchas de peregrino	lahs kohn-chahs deh peh-reh-gree-noh
shrimp	los camarones, las gambas	lohs kah-mah-roh-nehs, lahs gahm-bahs
sole	el lenguado	ehl lehn-gwah-doh

continues

Table 11.6 Fish and Seafood (El Pescado y Los Mariscos) (continued)

Fish or Seafood	Spanish	Pronunciation
swordfish	el pez espada	ehl pehs ehs-pah-dah
trout	la trucha	lah troo-chah
tuna	el atún	ehl ah-toon

Table 11.7 Dairy Products (Productos Lácteos)

Dairy Product	Spanish	Pronunciation
butter	la mantequilla	lah mahn-teh-kee-yah
cheese	el queso	ehl keh-soh
cream	la crema	lah kreh-mah
eggs	los huevos	lohs weh-bohs
yogurt	el yogur	ehl yoh-goohr

Table 11.8 Bakery Items (Pan y Postres)

Bread or Dessert	Spanish	Pronunciation
biscuit	el bizcocho	ehl bees-koh-choh
bread	el pan	ehl pahn
cake	el pastel	ehl pahs-tehl
cookie	la galleta	lah gah-yeh-tah
pie	el pastel	ehl pahs-tehl

Bread or Dessert	Spanish	Pronunciation
rice pudding	el arroz con leche	ehl ah-rohs kohn leh-cheh
rolls (sweet)	los panecillos (dulces)	lohs pah-neh-see-yohs (dool-sehs)

Table 11.9   Beverages (Las Bebidas)

Drink	Spanish	Pronunciation
beer	la cerveza	lah sehr-beh-sah
champagne	el champán	ehl chahm-pahn
cider	la sidra	lah see-drah
coffee (iced)	el café (helado)	ehl kah-feh (eh-lah-doh)
hot chocolate	el chocolate	ehl choh-koh-lah-teh
juice	el jugo	ehl hoo-goh
lemonade	la limonada	lah lee-moh-nah-dah
milk	la leche	lah leh-cheh
milkshake	el batido de leche	ehl bah-tee-doh deh leh-cheh
mineral water	el agua mineral	ehl ah-gwah mee-neh-rahl
carbonated	con gas	kohn gahs
noncarbonated	sin gas	seen gahs
soda	la gaseosa	lah gah-seh-yoh-sah
tea (iced)	el té (helado)	ehl teh (eh-lah-doh)
wine	el vino	ehl bee-noh

Getting the Right Amount

In Spanish-speaking countries, the metric system is used when measuring quantities of food. Liquids are measured in liters, and solids are measured in kilograms or fractions thereof. Most of us are used to dealing with ounces, pounds, pints, quarts, and gallons.

Not having been brought up on the metric system, I can understand that you might be a little confused. Sometimes it's just simpler to ask for a box, bag, jar, and so on, and to commit to memory the amounts we're accustomed to—a pound, a quart, and so on. Consult Table 11.10 to easily get the amount you want or need.

Table 11.10 Getting the Amount You Want

Amount	Spanish	Pronunciation
a bag of	un saco de	oon sah-koh deh
a bar of	una tableta de	oo-nah tah-bleh-tah deh
a bottle of	una botella de	oo-nah boh-teh-yah deh
a box of	una caja de	oo-nah kah-hah deh
a can of	una lata de	oo-nah lah-tah deh
a dozen	una docena de	oo-nah doh-seh-nah deh
a jar of	un pomo de	oon poh-moh deh
a package of	un paquete de	oon pah-keh-teh deh
a piece of	un pedazo de	oon peh-dah-soh deh
a slice of	un trozo de	oon troh-soh deh
a little	un poco de	oon poh-koh deh
a lot	mucho(a)	moo-choh(chah)

Amount	Spanish	Pronunciation
enough	bastante, suficiente	bahs-tahn-teh, soo-fee-see-yehn-teh
too much	demasiado	deh-mah-see-yah-doh

It's Mealtime

Breakfast, *el desayuno* (ehl deh-sah-yoo-noh), is generally eaten between 7 A.M. and 9 A.M. in Spanish-speaking countries. It usually is much lighter than its American counterpart, consisting of coffee with milk and bread with butter or jam. *Churros (choo-rohs)* (fritters made by frying long strips of dough in oil and then sprinkling them with sugar) and chocolate (hot chocolate) are special favorites.

Regional snacks and drinks (*batidas [bah-tee-dahs] y licuados [lee-kwah-dahs]*) that serve as midmorning snacks are consumed between 10:30 A.M. and noon.

Lunch, *la comida* (lah koh-mee-dah) in Spain and Mexico and *el almuerzo* (ehl ahl-mwehr-soh) in South America and the Caribbean, is eaten between 1:30 P.M. and 3:30 P.M., and is considered the main meal of the day. It includes soup, meat or fish, vegetables, salad, and dessert.

La merienda (lah meh-ree-yehn-dah), a late afternoon snack, is generally served between 5:00 P.M. and 6:00 P.M. It customarily consists of coffee or tea and pastry.

Supper is referred to as *la cena* (lah seh-nah) in Spain and as *la comida* (lah koh-mee-dah) in Spanish America. This meal tends to be light because it is consumed late, sometimes after 9:00 P.M.

Making Reservations

To make a reservation in a restaurant be sure to include the necessary information:

I would like to reserve a table …
Quisiera hacer una reserva …
kee-see-yeh-rah ah-sehr oo-nah rreh-sehr-bah

 … for this evening.
 para esta noche.
 pah-rah ehs-tah noh-cheh

 … for tomorrow evening.
 para mañana por la noche.
 pah-rah mah-nyah-nah pohr lah noh-cheh

 … for Saturday evening.
 para el sábado por la noche.
 pah-rah ehl sah-bah-doh pohr lah noh-cheh

 … for two people.
 para dos personas.
 pah-rah dohs pehr-soh-nahs

 … for 8:30 P.M.
 para las ocho y media.
 pah-rah lahs oh-choh ee meh-dee-yah

 … on the terrace, please (outdoors).
 en la terraza, por favor.
 ehn lah teh-rrah-sah pohr fah-bohr

… in the corner.
en el rincón.
ehn ehl rreen-kohn

… near the window.
cerca de la ventana.
sehr-kah deh lah behn-tah-nah

If you do not reserve a table and show up at a
restaurant unannounced, *el jefe de comedor* (ehl heh-
feh deh koh-meh-dohr), the "headwaiter," will
surely ask the following:

A table for how many?
¿Una mesa para cuántas personas?
oo-nah meh-sah pah-rah kwahn-tahs
pehr-soh-nahs

Make sure to answer his question completely, as
follows:

A table for two, please.
Una mesa para dos, por favor.
oo-nah meh-sah pah-rah dohs pohr fah-bohr

At the Table

Let's say you've now been seated. You look around
and are delighted with the fine china, the crystal,
the linen napkins, and the crisp white tablecloth. But
wait! Your fork is missing and a glass is chipped.
Table 11.11 provides the vocabulary you need when
asking the waiter for cutlery or other missing pieces.
Remember to say "*Necesito* …" (neh-seh-see-toh) to
tell the waiter what you need.

Table 11.11   Tableware (Servicio de Mesa)

Tableware	Spanish	Pronunciation
bowl	un tazón	oon tah-sohn
cup	una taza	oo-nah tah-sah
dinner plate	un plato	oon plah-toh
fork	un tenedor	oon teh-neh-dohr
glass	un vaso	oon bah-soh
knife	un cuchillo	oon koo-chee-yoh
menu	un menú	oon meh-noo
napkin	una servilleta	oo-nah sehr-bee-yeh-tah
place setting	un cubierto	oon koo-bee-yehr-toh
saucer	un platillo	oon plah-tee-yoh
soup dish	un sopero	oon soh-peh-roh
soup spoon	una cuchara	oo-nah koo-chah-rah
tablecloth	un mantel	oon mahn-tehl
teaspoon	una cucharita	oo-nah koo-chah-ree-tah
wine glass	una copa	oo-nah koh-pah

The waiter has come to give you a menu and to see whether you'd like a drink before dinner. You can use the following expressions for ordering both your food and drinks:

> What is today's specialty?
> *¿Cuál es el plato del día de hoy?*
> kwahl ehs ehl plah-toh dehl dee-yah deh oy

What is the house specialty?
¿Cuál es la especialidad de la casa?
kwahl ehs lah ehs-peh-see-yah-lee-dahd deh
lah kah-sah

What do you recommend?
¿Qué recomienda Ud.?
keh rreh-koh-mee-yehn-dah oo-stehd

I Need an Explanation

A Spanish menu can be confusing and overwhelming unless you know certain culinary terms. The waiter will probably get lost in his explanation. Table 11.12 gives you the terms you need to know for foods that are served primarily in Mexico.

Table 11.12   Understanding the Menu

Item	Pronunciation	Meaning
	Sauces (Salsas)	
ají de queso	ah-hee deh keh-soh	cheese sauce
adobo	ah-doh-boh	chili sauce made with sesame seeds, nuts, and spices
mole	moh-leh	chili sauce made with sesame seeds, cocoa, and spices
pipían	pee-pee-yahn	chili and pumpkin seed sauce spiced with coriander and served with bread crumbs

continues

Table 11.12 Understanding the Menu (continued)

Item	Pronunciation	Meaning
salsa cruda	sahl-sah kroo-dah	an uncooked tomato sauce dip
salsa de tomatilla	sahl-sah deh toh-mah-tee-yah	Mexican green tomato sauce
salsa de perejil	sahl-sah deh peh-reh-heel	parsley sauce
verde	behr-deh	green chili and green tomato sauce

Chilies (Chiles)

ancho	ahn-choh	medium hot
chipotle	chee-poh-tehl	hot, smokey-flavored
jalapeño	hah-lah-peh-nyoh	hot, meaty-flavored
pasilla	pah-see-yah	hot, rich, sweet-flavored
pequín	peh-keen	hot
pimiento	pee-mee-yehn-toh	peppery
poblano	poh-blah-noh	medium hot, rich-flavored
serrano	seh-rrah-noh	hot

Tortillas (Tortillas)

burrito	boo-ree-toh	flour tortilla with a cheese and meat filling and served with salsa
chalupas	chah-loo-pahs	cheese- or ground pork–filled tortillas served with a green chili sauce

Item	Pronunciation	Meaning
chilaquiles	chee-lah-kee-lehs	baked layers of tortillas filled alternately with beans, meat, chicken, and cheese
enchiladas	ehn-chee-lah-dahs	soft corn tortillas filled with meat, rice, and cheese and topped with spicy sauce
flautas	flow-tahs	rolled, flute-shaped, deep-fried tortilla sandwiches
quesadillas	keh-sah-dee-yahs	deep-fried tortillas covered with cheese, tomato, and pepper
tacos	tah-kohs	crisp toasted tortillas filled with meat, poultry, or beans and topped with shredded lettuce, cheese, and sauce
tostada	tohs-tah-dah	tortilla chips with different pepper and cheese toppings

Appetizers (Los Aperitivos)

alcachofas	ahl-kah-choh-fahs	artichokes
almejas	ahl-meh-hahs	clams
anguilas	ahn-gee-lahs	smoked eels
ahumadas	ah-oo-mah-dahs	smoked
calamares	kah-lah-mah-rehs	squid

continues

Table 11.12 Understanding the Menu
(continued)

Item	Pronunciation	Meaning
camarones	kah-mah-roh-nehs	shrimp
caracoles	kah-rah-koh-lehs	snails
champiñones	chahm-pee-nyoh-nehs	mushrooms
chorizo	choh-ree-soh	spicy sausage
cigales	see-gah-lehs	crayfish
guacamole	gwah-kah-moh-leh	avocado spread
huevos	hweh-bohs	eggs
melón	meh-lohn	melon
moluscos	moh-loos-kohs	mussels
ostras	ohs-trahs	oysters
sardinas	sahr-dee-nahs	sardines
tostadas	tohs-tah-dahs	tortilla chips

Soups (Las Sopas)

gazpacho	gahs-pah-choh	puréed uncooked vegetable soup, served cold
potaje madrileño	poh-tah-heh mah-dree-leh-nyoh	thick, puréed cod, spinach, and chick peas
sopa de ajo	soh-pah deh ah-hoh	garlic soup
sopa de albóndigas	soh-pah deh ahl-bohn-dee-gahs	meatball soup
sopa de cebolla	soh-pah deh seh-boh-lah	onion soup
sopa de fideos	soh-pah deh fee-deh-yohs	noodle soup

Item	Pronunciation	Meaning
sopa de gambas	soh-pah deh gahm-bahs	shrimp soup
sopa de mariscos	soh-pah deh mah-rees-kohs	seafood soup
sopa de pescado	soh-pah deh pehs-kah-doh	fish soup
sopa de verduras	soh-pah deh behr-doo-rahs	soup made from puréed green vegetables

Proper Preparation

Of course, you want to make sure your meal is cooked just the way you like it. The waiter may ask the following:

> How do you want it (them)?
> *¿Cómo lo (los, la, las) quiere?*
> koh-moh loh (lohs, lah, lahs) kee-yeh-reh

Table 11.13 will help you express your wants and needs.

Table 11.13 Preparing It Properly

Term	Spanish	Pronunciation
baked	asado	ah-sah-doh
boiled	hervido	ehr-bee-doh
breaded	empanado	ehm-pah-nah-doh

continues

Table 11.13 Preparing It Properly (continued)

Term	Spanish	Pronunciation
broiled	a la parrilla	ah lah pah-rree-yah
browned	al horno	ahl ohr-noh
chopped	picado	pee-kah-doh
fried	frito	free-toh
grilled	asado a la parrilla	ah-sah-doh ah lah pah-rree-yah
marinated	escabechado	ehs-kah-beh-chah-doh
mashed	puré	poo-reh
poached	escalfado	ehs-kahl-fah-doh
roasted	asado	ah-sah-doh
with sauce	con salsa	kohn sahl-sah
sautéed	salteado	sahl-teh-yah-doh
smoked	ahumado	ah-oo-mah-doh
steamed	al vapor	ahl bah-pohr
stewed	estofado	ehs-toh-fah-doh
very rare	casi crudo	kah-see kroo-doh
rare	poco asado	poh-koh ah-sah-doh
medium rare	un poco rojo pero no crudo	oon poh-koh rroh-hoh peh-roh noh kroo-doh
medium	a término medio	ah tehr-mee-noh meh-dee-yoh
well-done	bien asado (hecho, cocido)	bee-yehn ah-sah-doh (eh-choh, koh-see-doh)

Eggs (Los Huevos)

fried	fritos	free-tohs
hard-boiled	duros	doo-rohs

Term	Spanish	Pronunciation
poached	escalfados	ehs-kahl-fah-dohs
scrambled	revueltos	rreh-bwehl-tohs
soft-boiled	pasados por agua	pah-sah-dohs pohr ah-gwah
omelet	una tortilla	oo-nah tohr-tee-yah
plain omelet	una tortilla francesa	oo-nah tohr-tee-yah frahn-seh-sah
herb omelet	una tortilla con hierbas	oo-nah tohr-tee-yah kohn yehr-bahs

Spice It Up

Different spices are used in Spain and in the Spanish-American countries. Depend on menu descriptions or your server to help you determine whether the dish will be to your liking—bland or spicy. Table 11.14 will help you with the spices you might encounter.

Table 11.14 Herbs, Spices, and Condiments (Hierbas, Especias, y Condimentos)

Term	Spanish	Pronunciation
basil	la albahaca	lah ahl-bah-ah-kah
butter	la mantequilla	lah mahn-teh-kee-yeh
dill	el eneldo	ehl eh-nehl-doh
garlic	el ajo	ehl ah-hoh
ginger	el jenjibre	ehl hehn-hee-breh
honey	la miel	lah mee-yehl

continues

Table 11.14 Herbs, Spices, and Condiments (Hierbas, Especias, y Condimentos) (continued)

Term	Spanish	Pronunciation
jam, jelly	la mermelada	lah mehr-meh-lah-dah
ketchup	la salsa de tomate	lah sahl-sah deh toh-mah-teh
lemon	el limón	ehl lee-mohn
mayonnaise	la mayonesa	lah meh-yoh-neh-sah
mustard	la mostaza	lah mohs-tah-sah
oil	el aceite	ehl ah-seh-ee-teh
oregano	el orégano	ehl oh-reh-gah-noh
paprika	el pimentón dulce	ehl pee-mehn-tohn dool-seh
parsley	el perejil	ehl peh-reh-heel
pepper	la pimienta	lah pee-mee-yehn-tah
rosemary	el romero	ehl rroh-meh-roh
saffron	el azafrán	ehl ah-sah-frahn
salt	la sal	lah sahl
sesame	el ajonjolí	ehl ah-hohn-hoh-lee
sugar	el azúcar	ehl ah-soo-kahr
thyme	el tomillo	ehl toh-mee-yoh
vinegar	el vinagre	ehl bee-nah-greh

¡Cuidado!

There is no Spanish word for "some" when the item/amount can't be counted. Use *quisiera* (kee-see-yeh-rah) + the noun to express what you want, as follows:

> *Quisisera sal, por favor.*
> I'd like some salt, please.

Special Requests

If you have certain likes, dislikes, or dietary restrictions that you would like to make known, keep the phrases in Table 11.15 handy.

Table 11.15   Dietary Restrictions

Phrase	Spanish	Pronunciation
I am on a diet.	Estoy a régimen.	ehs-toy ah rreh-hee-mehn
I'm a vegetarian.	Soy vegetariano(a).	soy beh-heh-tah-ree-yah-noh(nah)
I can't have …	No puedo tomar …	noh pweh-doh toh-mahr
any dairy products	productos lácteos	proh-dook-tohs lahk-teh-yohs
any alcohol	alcohol	ahl-koh-ohl
any saturated fats	grasas saturadas	grah-sahs sah-too-rah-dahs
any shellfish	mariscos	mah-rees-kohs

continues

Table 11.15 Dietary Restrictions (continued)

Phrase	Spanish	Pronunciation
I'm looking for a dish ...	Estoy buscando un plato ...	ehs-toy boos-kahn-doh oon plah-toh
high in fiber	con mucha fibra	kohn moo-chah fee-brah
low in cholesterol	con poco colesterol	kohn poh-koh koh-lehs-teh-rohl
low in fat	con poca grasa	kohn poh-kah grah-sah
low in sodium	con poca sal	kohn poh-kah sahl
nondairy	no lácteo	noh lahk-teh-yoh
salt-free	sin sal	seen sahl
sugar-free	sin azúcar	seen ah-soo-kahr
without artificial coloring	sin colorantes artificiales	seen koh-loh-rah-tehs ahr-tee-fee-see-yah-lehs
without preservatives	sin preservativos	seen preh-sehr-bah-tee-bohs

Please Take It Back to the Kitchen

At times, the cooking or the table setting might not be up to your standards. Table 11.16 presents some problems you might encounter.

Table 11.16   Possible Problems

Term	Spanish	Pronunciation
It's cold.	Está frío.	ehs-tah free-yoh
It's too rare.	Está demasiado crudo.	ehs-tah deh-mah-see-yah-doh kroo-doh
It's over-cooked.	Está sobrecocido.	ehs-tah soh-breh-koh-see-doh
It's burned.	Está quemado.	ehs-tah keh-mah-doh
It's too salty.	Está muy salado.	ehs-tah mwee sah-lah-doh
It's too sweet.	Está muy dulce.	ehs-tah mwee dool-seh
It's too spicy.	Está demasiado picante.	ehs-tah deh-mah see-yah-doh pee-kahn-teh
It's bitter (sour).	Está agrio (cortado).	ehs-tah ah-gree-yoh (kohr-tah-doh)
It's dirty.	Está sucio.	ehs-tah soo-see-yoh

Fancy Endings

When it's time for dessert, choose from among the delightful specialties in Table 11.17.

Table 11.17   Daring Desserts

Dessert	In Spanish	Pronunciation
caramel custard	el flan	ehl flahn
cookies	las galletas	lahs gah-yeh-tahs

continues

Table 11.17   Daring Desserts   (continued)

Dessert	In Spanish	Pronunciation
ice cream	el helado	ehl eh-lah-doh
pie	el pastel	ehl pahs-tehl
sponge cake	el bizcocho	ehl bees-koh-choh
tart	la tarta	lah tahr-tah
yogurt	el yogur	ehl yoh-goor

Table 11.18   Ice Cream

cone	un barquillo	oon bahr-kee-yoh
cup	una copa	oo-nah koh-pah
chocolate	de chocolate	deh choh-koh-lah-teh
vanilla	de vainilla	deh bah-ee-nee-yah
strawberry	de fresa	deh freh-sah
pistachio	de pistacho	deh pees-tah-choh

Table 11.19   Wine

red wine	el vino tinto	ehl bee-noh teen-toh
rosé wine	el vino rosado	ehl bee-noh rroh-sah-doh
white wine	el vino blanco	ehl bee-noh blahn-koh
dry wine	el vino seco	ehl bee-noh seh-koh
sweet wine	el vino dulce	ehl bee-noh dool-seh
sparkling wine	el vino espumoso	ehl bee-noh ehs-poo-moh-soh
champagne	el champán	ehl chahm-pahn

Chapter 12

Being Sociable

In This Chapter

- Amusements and diversions
- Invitations: extending, accepting, and refusing

Are you heading off to the sea to engage in water sports, up to the mountains for skiing or hiking, onto the links for a round of golf, or onto the courts for a brisk tennis match? Are you a film buff or a theatergoer? Do you enjoy a lively opera or an elegant ballet? Perhaps the game's the thing, and you'll spend some time with a one-armed bandit in a luxurious casino. With the help of this chapter, you'll be able to do it all—whether you're the guest or the one doing the inviting.

I Live for Sports

Whether you like to relax as a beach bum, spend your days gazing out at the azure ocean, or feel compelled to engage in every fast-paced sport you can, you need certain words and terms to make your preferences known. Table 12.1 provides a list of sports and outdoor activities. The verbs *hacer** and *jugar + a +* definite article** (*el, la, los, las*) are often used to show participation in the sports indicated with asterisks below. Any verb indicated in parentheses is used in place of *jugar* or *hacer.*

I (don't) like …	I (don't) like …
(one sport)	(more than one sport)
(No) Me gusta …	*(No) Me gustan …*
(noh) meh goos-tah …	(noh) meh goos-tahn …

I want to play …
Quiero jugar + a + definite article …
kee-yeh-roh hoo-gahr ah

or

Quiero hacer …
kee-yeh-roh ah-sehr

The verb *querer* is irregular and can be followed by the infinitive of a verb:

yo	*quiero*	kee-yeh-roh
tú	*quieres*	kee-yeh-rehs
él, ella, Ud.	*quiere*	kee-yeh-reh
nosotros	*queremos*	keh-reh-mohs
vosotros	*queréis*	keh-reh-ees
ellos, ellas, Uds.	*quieren*	kee-yeh-rehn

We want to play golf.
Nosotros queremos jugar al golf.
nohs-oh-trohs keh-reh-mohs hoo-gahr ahl gohlf

Table 12.1   Sports

Sport	Spanish	Pronunciation
aerobics	los aeróbicos*	lohs ah-yeh-roh-bee-kohs
baseball	el beísbol**	ehl beh-ees-bohl
basketball	el baloncesto**, el básquetbol**	ehl bah-lohn-sehs-toh, ehl bahs-keht-bohl
bicycling	el ciclismo* (montar a bicicleta)	ehl see-klees-moh (mohn-tahr ah bee-see-kleh-tah)
body-building	el culturismo*	ehl kool-too-rees-moh
fishing	la pesca (ir de pesca)	lah pehs-kah (eer deh pehs-kah)
golf	el golf**	ehl gohlf
horseback riding	la equitación*	lah eh-kee-tah-see-yohn
jogging	el footing* (trotar)	ehl foo-teeng (troh-tahr)
sailing	la navegación* (navegar)	lah nah-beh-gah-see-yohn (nah-beh-gahr)
scuba (skin) diving	el buceo (bucear)	ehl boo-seh-yoh (boo-seh-ahr)
soccer	el fútbol**	ehl foot-bohl
surfing	el surf* (surfear)	ehl soorf (soor-feh-yahr)
swimming	la natación* (nadar)	lah nah-tah-see-yohn (nah-dahr)
tennis	el tenis**	ehl teh-nees
volleyball	el volíbol**	ehl boh-lee-bohl
water-skiing	el esquí acuático*	ehl ehs-kee ah-kwah-tee-koh

The verbs *jugar** and *hacer***, used with the sports indicated in the table above, are irregular:

Jugar (hoo-gahr)

yo juego	(hweh-goh)
nosotros jugamos	(hoo-gah-mohs)
tú juegas	(hweh-gahs)
vosotros jugáis	(hoo-gah-ees)
él, ella, Ud. juega	(hweh-gah)
ellos, ellas, Uds. juegan	(hweh-gahn)

Hacer (ah-sehr)

yo hago	(ah-goh)
nosotros hacemos	(ah-seh-mohs)
tú haces	(ah-sehs)
vosotros hacéis	(ah-seh-ees)
él, ella, Ud. hace	(ah-seh)
ellos, ellas, Uds. hacen	(ah-sehn)

Sports Equipment

You went on vacation but didn't trust the airlines with your golf clubs and tennis rackets. Or you thought you wouldn't want to play, but now you've changed your mind. You can still enjoy your favorite sport if you borrow or rent equipment. Use these phrases when you find yourself in a similar predicament:

I need …	
Me falta(n) …	*Necesito* …
meh fahl-tah(n)	neh-seh-see-toh

Could you lend (rent) me ...?
Podría Ud. prestarme (alquilarme) ...?
poh-dree-yah oo-stehd prehs-tahr-meh
(ahl-kee-lahr-meh)

Table 12.2 Sports Equipment (El Equipo Deportivo)

Equipment	Spanish	Pronunciation
ball (football, soccer)	la bola	lah boh-lah
ball (baseball, jai alai, tennis)	la pelota	lah peh-loh-tah
ball (basketball)	el balón	ehl bah-lohn
bat	el bate	ehl bah-teh
bicycle	la bicicleta	lah bee-see-kleh-tah
boat	el barco	ehl bahr-koh
canoe	la canoa	lah kah-noh-wah
diving suit	la escafandra	lah ehs-kah-fahn-drah
fishing rod	la caña de pesca	lah kah-nyah deh pehs-kah
golf clubs	los palos de golf	lohs pah-lohs deh gohlf
net	la red	lah rrehd
racquet	la raqueta	lah rrah-keh-tah
skates	los patines	lohs pah-tee-nehs
skis	los esquís	lohs ehs-kees
surfboard	el acuaplano	ehl ah-kwah-plah-noh

Other Amusements

Perhaps sports aren't part of your agenda. There are plenty of other activities you can pursue to have a good time. The phrases in Table 12.3 give you the tools to make many other intriguing suggestions. Should you delight in going to the opera, the ballet, the theater, or a concert, don't forget to bring along *los gemelos* (lohs heh-meh-lohs), "binoculars."

Table 12.3   Places to Go

El Lugar (ehl loo-gahr)	Pronunciation	The Place
ir a la ópera	eer a lah oh-peh-rah	go to the opera
ir a la playa	eer ah lah plah-yah	go to the beach
Ir a una discoteca	eer ah oon-ah dees-koh-the-kah	go to a disco
ir a un ballet	eer ah oon bah-leh	go to a ballet
ir a un casino	eer ah oon kah-see-noh	go to a casino
ir al centro comercial	eer al sehn-troh koh-mehr-see-yahl	go to the mall
ir al cine	eer al see-neh	go to the movies
ir a un conci-erto	eer ah oon kohn-see-yehr-toh	go to a concert
ir al teatro	eer al teh-yah-troh	go to the theater
quedarse en su habitación (casa)	keh-dahr-seh ehn soo ah-bee-tah-see-yohn (kah-sah)	stay in one's room (home)

At the Movies and on Television

Do you crave some quiet relaxation? Is the weather bad? Do you feel like getting away from everyone and everything? There's always a movie or the television. It seems that cable has invaded the planet and can accommodate anyone who needs a few carefree hours. If you want to be entertained, consult Table 12.4 for the possibilities.

What kind of film are they showing?
¿Qué tipo de película están dando?
keh tee-poh deh peh-lee-koo-lah ehs-tahn dahn-doh

What's on television?
¿Qué hay en la televisión?
keh ahy ehn lah teh-leh-bee-see-yohn

Table 12.4   Movies and Television Programs

Program Type	Spanish	Pronunciation
adventure film	una película de aventura	oo-nah peh-lee-koo-lah deh ah-behn-too-rah
cartoons	los dibujos animados	lohs dee-boo-hohs ah-nee-mah-dohs
comedy	una comedia	oo-nah koh-meh-dee-yah
game show	un juego	oon hweh-goh
horror movie	una película de horror	oo-nah peh-lee-koo-lah deh oh-rrohr
love story	una película de amor	oo-nah peh-lee-koo-lah deh ah-mohr

continues

Table 12.4 Movies and Television Programs (continued)

Program Type	Spanish	Pronunciation
mystery	un misterio	oon mees-teh-ree-yoh
news	las noticias	lahs noh-tee-see-yahs
police story	una película policiaca	oo-nah peh-lee-koo-lah poh-lee-see-yah-kah
science-fiction film	una película deciencia ficción	oo-nah peh-lee-koo-lah deh see-yehn-see-yah feek-see-yohn
soap opera	una tele-novela	oo-nah teh-leh-noh-beh-lah
spy movie	una película de espía	oo-nah peh-lee-koo-lah deh ehs-pee-yah
talk show	un programa de entrevistas	oon proh-grah-mah deh ehn-treh-bees-tahs
weather	el parte meteoro-lógico, el pronóstico	ehl pahr-teh meh-teh-yoh-roh-loh-hee-koh, ehl proh-nohs-tee-koh

Refer to the following explanations when you choose a movie or theater:

> Forbidden for those under 18 unless accompanied by an adult.
> *Prohibida para menores de 18 años a menos de que esté acompañado por un adulto.*

> You must be older than 13.
> *Mayores de 13 años.*

> Original version, subtitled.
> *Versión original.*

Dubbed in Spanish.
Versión doblada al español.

Reduced rate.
Tarifa reducida.

So What Did You Think?

If you enjoy the program, you might say the following:

Phrase	Spanish	Pronunciation
I love it!	¡Me encanta!	meh ehn-kahn-tah
It's a good movie.	Es una buena película.	ehs oo-nah bweh-nah peh-lee-koo-lah
It's amusing!	¡Es divertida!	ehs dee-behr-tee-dah
It's great!	¡Es fantástica!	ehs fahn-tahs-tee-kah
It's moving!	¡Me conmueve!	meh kohn-moo-weh-beh
It's original!	¡Es original!	ehs oh-ree-hee-nahl

If the show leaves something to be desired, try the following phrases:

Phrase	Spanish	Pronunciation
I hate it!	¡La odio!	lah oh-dee-yoh
It's a bad movie!	¡Es una mala película!	ehs oo-nah mah-lah peh-lee-koo-lah
It's a loser!	¡Es un desastre!	ehs oon deh-sahs-treh
It's garbage!	¡Es basura!	ehs bah-soo-rah

continues

continued

Phrase	Spanish	Pronunciation
It's the same old thing!	¡Siempre es lo mismo!	see-yehm-preh ehs loh mees-moh
It's too violent!	¡Es demasiado violenta!	ehs deh-mah-see-yah-doh bee-yoh-lehn-tah

Invitations

It isn't much fun to play alone. Why not ask someone to join you? To extend an invitation, you can ask the following:

> Do you want to join me (us)?
> *¿Quiere (Quieres) acompañarme (acompañarnos)?*
> kee-yeh-reh (kee-yeh-rehs) ah-kohm-pah-nyahr-meh (ah-kohm-pah-nyahr-nohs)

Whether you've been invited to participate in a sport or an outing, to visit a museum, or just to stay at someone's home, the following phrases will allow you to graciously accept, to cordially refuse, or to show your indifference:

Phrase	Spanish	Pronunciation
Accepting		
Gladly.	Con placer.	kohn plah-sehr
Great!	¡Magnífico!	mahg-nee-fee-koh
If you want to.	Si tú quieres. (Ud. quiere.)	see too kee-yeh-rehs (oo-stehd kee-yeh-reh)
Okay. (I agree.)	De acuerdo.	deh ah-kwehr-doh

Phrase	Spanish	Pronunciation
Of course.	Por supuesto.	pohr soo-pwehs-toh
That's a good idea.	Es una buena idea.	ehs oo-nah bweh-nah ee-deh-yah
Why not?	¿Por qué no?	pohr keh noh
With pleasure.	Con mucho gusto.	kohn moo-choh goos-toh

Refusing

I'm busy.	Estoy ocupado.	ehs-toy oh-koo-pah-doh
I'm sorry.	Lo siento.	loh see-yehn-toh
I'm tired.	Estoy cansado.	ehs-toy kahn-sah-doh
I can't.	No puedo.	noh pweh-doh
I don't feel like it.	No tengo ganas.	noh tehn-goh gah-nahs
I don't want to.	No quiero.	noh kee-yeh-roh
Not again!	¿Otra vez?	oh-trah behs

Showing Indifference

I don't have any preference.	No tengo preferencia.	noh tehn-goh preh-feh-rehn-see-yah
I don't know.	Yo no sé.	yoh noh seh
It depends.	Depende.	deh-peh-deh
Perhaps. Maybe.	Tal vez.	tahl behs
Whatever you want.	Lo que Ud. prefiera (tú prefieras).	loh keh oo-stehd preh-fee-yeh-rah (too preh-fee-yeh-rahs)

Personal Care

In This Chapter

- At the hairdresser's
- At the dry cleaner's
- At the laundromat
- At the shoemaker's
- At the optician's
- At the jeweler's
- At the camera shop
- Other services

You've been traveling and having a wonderful time. All of a sudden, you have a problem that just can't wait—your roots have surfaced in record time, you spilled tomato sauce on your new white silk shirt, you dropped your contact lens down the drain, you lost a heel on your shoe, or your 4-year-old has dropped your camera in the bathtub. You're not home, and you're hesitant about what to do. Don't worry. You just have to know what to say to get the job done. Ask for *las páginas amarillas* (lahs pah-hee-nahs ah-mah-ree-yahs, the Yellow Pages), read the ads, and then explain your problem.

What a Bad Hair Day!

In the past, men went to a *barbería* (bahr-beh-ree-yah, a barber's), whereas women went to a *salón de belleza* (sah-lohn deh beh-yeh-sah, a beauty parlor). Today these establishments have become more or less unisex, with men and women demanding more or less the same services. To get what you want simply ask the following:

Could you give me ...	I would like ...
Podría darme ...	*Quisiera ...*
poh-dree-yah dahr-meh	kee-see-yeh-rah

Today's salons provide the services listed in Table 13.1.

Table 13.1 Hair and Salon Care

Term	Spanish	Pronunciation
a haircut	un corte de pelo	oon kohr-teh deh peh-loh
a manicure	una manicura	oo-nah mah-nee-koo-rah
a pedicure	una pedicura	oo-nah peh-dee-koo-rah
a permanent	una permanente	oo-nah pehr-mah-nehn-teh
a rinse	un aclarado colorante	oon ah-klah-rah-doh koh-loh-rahn-teh
a set	un marcado	oon mahr-kah-doh
a shampoo	un champú	oon chahm-poo
a trim	un recorte	oon rreh-kohr-teh
a waxing	una depilación	oo-nah deh-pee-lah-see-yohn
highlights	reflejos	rreh-fleh-hohs

Term	Spanish	Pronunciation
layers	un corte en capas	oon kohr-teh ehn kah-pahs

Do you need other services? Table 13.2 provides the phrases you need to get them. Use the following phrases to preface your request:

> Could you ... please
> *Podría Ud. ... por favor*
> poh-dree-yah oo-stehd ... pohr fah-bohr

Table 13.2   Other Services

Service	Spanish	Pronunciation
blow dry my hair	secarme el pelo	seh-kahr-meh ehl peh-loh
curl my hair	rizarme el pelo	rree-sahr-meh ehl peh-loh
shave my beard my mustache my head	afeitarme la barba el bigote la cabeza	ah-feh-ee-tahr-meh lah bahr-bah ehl bee-goh-teh lah kah-beh-sah
straighten my hair	estirarme el pelo	ehs-tee-rahr-meh ehl peh-loh
trim my bangs	recortarme el flequillo	rreh-kohr-tahr-meh ehl fleh-kee-yoh
trim my beard my mustache my sideburns	recortarme la barba el bigote las patillas	rreh-kohr-tahr-meh lah bahr-bah ehl bee-goh-teh lahs pah-tee-yahs

Getting What You Want

It's hard enough getting the haircut and style you want when there is no language barrier—imagine the disasters that could befall your poor mop in a foreign country! The following phrases will help make your styling and coloring preferences clear to your *peinador* (peh-ee-nah-dor, hairstylist):

> I prefer my hair …
> *Prefiero mi pelo …*
> preh-fee-yeh-roh mee peh-loh

> I'd like a … style.
> *Quisiera un peinado …*
> kee-see-yeh-rah oon peh-ee-nah-doh

Style	Spanish	Pronunciation
long	largo	lahr-goh
medium	mediano	meh-dee-yah-noh
short	corto	kohr-toh
wavy	ondulado	ohn-doo-lah-doh
curly	rizado	rree-sah-doh
straight	lacio (liso)	lah-see-yoh (lee-soh)

If you don't want certain products on your hair, don't be afraid to tell the hairdresser.

> Don't put on any … please
> *No me ponga … por favor*
> noh meh pohn-gah … pohr fah-bohr

Product	Spanish	Pronunciation
conditioner	suavizante	swah-bee-sahn-teh
gel	gomina, gelatina	goh-mee-nah, geh-lah-tee-nah
hairspray	laca	lah-kah
lotion	loción	loh-see-yohn
mousse	espuma	ehs-poo-mah
shampoo	champú	chahm-poo

Don't forget to ask about tipping:

> Is the tip included?
> *¿Está incluida la propina?*
> ehs-tah een-kloo-wee-dah lah proh-pee-nah

Problems in General

The following phrases will come in handy when you are seeking certain services or are trying to have something repaired. Use them at the dry cleaner, the shoemaker, the optician, the jeweler, or the camera store:

> At what time do you open (close)?
> *¿A qué hora abre (cierra) Ud.?*
> ah keh oh-rah ah-breh (see-yeh-reh) oo-sted

> What days are you open (closed)?
> *¿Qué días está Ud. abierto (cerrado)?*
> keh dee-yahs ehs-tah oo-stehd ah-bee-yehr-toh (seh-rah-doh)

Can you fix it (them) today?
¿Puede Ud. arreglármelo (la, los, las) hoy?
pweh-deh oo-stehd ah-rreh-glahr-meh-loh
(lah, lohs, lahs) oy

Can you fix it (them) temporarily (while I wait)?
*¿Puede Ud. arreglármelo (la, los, las) temporal-
mente (mientras yo espero)?*
pweh-deh oo-stehd ah-rreh-glahr-meh-loh
(lah, lohs, lahs) tehm-poh-rahl-mehn-teh
(mee-yehn-trahs yoh ehs-peh-roh)

How long do I have to wait?
¿Cuánto tiempo tengo que esperar?
kwahn-toh tee-yehm-poh tehn-goh keh
ehs-peh-rahr

How much do I owe you?
¿Cuánto le debo?
kwahn-toh leh deh-boh

Do you accept credit cards (traveler's checks)?
¿Acepta tarjetas de crédito (cheques de viajero)?
ah-sehp-tah tahr-heh-tahs deh kreh-dee-toh
(cheh-kehs deh bee-yah-heh-roh)

May I have a receipt?
¿Me puede dar un recibo?
meh pweh-deh dahr oon rreh-see-boh

At the Dry Cleaner's

You've unpacked. Your white shirt looks like you
slept in it, and your beige pants have an ugly stain
you hadn't noticed before. Don't fret. Your stains,

spots, tears, and wrinkles can be taken care of if you
know how to explain your problem and how to ask
for the necessary service:

I have a problem. There is (are) ...
Tengo un problema. *Hay ...*
tehn-goh oon proh-bleh-mah ahy

Phrase	Spanish	Pronunciation
a hole	un hueco	oon weh-koh
a missing button	un botón perdido	oon boh-tohn pehr-dee-doh
missing buttons	botones perdidos	boh-toh-nehs pehr-dee-dohs
a spot, a stain	una mancha	oo-nah mahn-chah

Now that you've explained the problem, state what
you'd like done about it:

Can you (dry) clean this (these) ... for me?
¿Puede Ud. lavarme este (esta, estos, estas) ... (en seco)?
pweh-deh oo-stehd lah-bahr-meh ehs-teh
(ehs-tah, ehs-tohs, ehs-tahs) ... (ehn seh-koh)

Can you please mend this (these) ... for me?
¿Puede Ud. remendarme este (esta, estos, estas) ...?
pweh-deh oo-stehd rreh-mehn-dahr-meh
ehs-teh (ehs-tah, ehs-tohs, ehs-tahs)

Can you please press (starch) this (these) ... for me?
¿Puede Ud. plancharme (almidonarme) este (esta, estos, estas) ...?
pweh-deh oo-stehd plahn-chahr-meh (ahl-mee-doh-nahr-meh) ehs-teh (ehs-tah, ehs-tohs, ehs-tahs)

I need it (them) …
Lo (la, los, las) necesito …
loh (lah, lohs, lahs) neh-seh-see-toh …

today.	tomorrow.
hoy.	*mañana.*
oy	mah-nyah-nah
this afternoon.	the day after tomorrow.
esta tarde.	*pasado mañana.*
ehs-tah tahr-deh	pah-sah-doh mah-nyah-nah
tonight.	next week.
esta noche.	*la semana próxima.*
ehs-tah noh-cheh	lah seh-mah-nah prohk-see-mah

Something Extra

If you want a service performed for yourself or someone else, use the appropriate indirect object: *me* (for me), *te* (for you), *le* (for him or her), *nos* (for us), *os* (for you), *les* (for them).

Can you please mend this pair of pants for him (her)?
¿Puede Ud. tejerle este pantalón?
pweh-deh oo-stehd teh-hahr-leh ehs-the pahn-tah-lohn

At the Laundromat

If your laundry has piled up and you don't mind doing it yourself, you might try to seek out a laundromat. Use the following phrases to get the information you need:

I'd like to clean my clothes.
Quiero limpiarme la ropa.
kee-yeh-roh leem-pee-yahr-meh lah rroh-pah

I'd like to have my clothes washed.
Quiero que me laven la ropa.
kee-yeh-roh keh meh lah-behn lah rroh-pah

If you want to do the job yourself, the following phrases might serve you well:

Is there a free (unoccupied) washing machine (dryer)?
¿Hay una máquina de lavar (secadora) libre?
ahy oo-nah mah-kee-nah deh lah-bahr
(seh-kah-doh-rah) lee-breh

Where can I buy soap powder?
¿Dónde puedo comprar jabón en polvo?
dohn-deh pweh-doh kohm-prahr hah-bohn
ehn pohl-boh

I need bleach.
Necesito lejía.
neh-seh-see-toh leh-hee-yah

At the Shoemaker's

Let's say you've walked so much you've worn down the soles of your shoes. Perhaps you've broken a shoelace on your dress shoes or you just want a shine.

The following phrases will help you describe your problem:

> Can you repair … for me?
> *¿Puede Ud. remendarme …?*
> pweh-deh oo-stehd rreh-mehn-dahr-meh

these shoes	this heel
estos zapatos	*este tacón*
ehs-tohs sah-pah-tohs	ehs-teh tah-kohn
these boots	this sole
estas botas	*esta suela*
ehs-tahs boh-tahs	ehs-tah sweh-lah

> Do you sell shoelaces?
> *¿Vende Ud. cordones de zapato?*
> behn-deh oo-stehd kohr-doh-nehs deh
> sah-pah-toh

> When can I have them?
> *¿Cuándo los tendrá?*
> kwahn-doh lohs tehn-drah

> I need them by Tuesday (without fail).
> *Los necesito para el martes (sin falta).*
> lohs neh-seh-see-toh pah-rah ehl mahr-tehs
> (seen fahl-tah)

At the Optician's

What could be more annoying than losing or tearing a contact lens or breaking or losing a pair of glasses while away from home? For people who depend on these optical necessities, the following phrases could one day prove useful:

Can you repair these glasses for me?
¿Puede Ud. arreglarme estos lentes (estas gafas)?
pweh-deh oo-stehd ah-rreh-glahr-meh ehs-tohs
lehn-tehs (ehs-tahs gah-fahs)

Can you tighten the screws?
¿Puede apretar los tornillitos?
pweh-deh ah-preh-tahr lohs tohr-nee-yee-tohs

I need the glasses immediately.
Necesito las gafas inmediatamente.
neh-seh-see-toh lahs gah-fahs
een-meh-dee-yah-tah-mehn-the

Can you replace this contact lens?
¿Puede Ud. darme otra lentilla (otro lente) de contacto?
pweh-deh oo-stehd dahr-meh oh-trah lehn-tee-
yah (oh-troh lehn-teh) deh kohn-tahk-toh

Do you sell sunglasses?
¿Vende Ud. lentes (gafas) de sol?
behn-deh oo-stehd lehn-tehs (gah-fahs) deh sohl

At the Jeweler's

If your watch has stopped or isn't working as it
should, you might find it necessary to have it
repaired before returning home.

My watch doesn't work.
Mi reloj no funciona.
mee rreh-loh noh foon-see-yoh-nah

My watch has stopped.
Mi reloj está parado.
mee rreh-loh ehs-tah pah-rah-doh

My watch is fast (slow).
Mi reloj se adelanta (se atrasa).
mee rreh-loh seh ah-deh-lahn-tah (seh ah-trah-sah)

When will it be ready?
¿Cuándo estará listo?
kwahn-doh ehs-tah-rah lees-toh

Do you sell bands (batteries)?
¿Vende Ud. pulseras (baterías)?
behn-deh oo-stehd pool-seh-rahs (bah-teh-ree-yahs)

At the Camera Shop

For many people, a vacation is not a vacation unless they capture it on film. If you need to visit a camera shop or a film store in a Spanish-speaking country, the following words and phrases will come in handy:

Term	Spanish	Pronunciation
a camera	una cámara	oo-nah kah-mah-rah
film	una película	oo-nah peh-lee-koo-lah
a video camera	una videocámara	oo-nah bee-deh-yoh-kah-mah-rah
a digital camera	una cámara digital	oo-nah kah-mah-rah dee-hee-tahl
a storage card	un soporte de almacenamiento	oon soh-pohr-teh deh ahl-mah-seh-nah-mee-yehn-toh

If you have special needs, you might ask:

>Can you fix this camera?
>*¿Puede arreglar esta cámara?*
>pweh-deh ah-rreh-glahr ehs-tah kah-mah-rah

>How much will the repair cost?
>*¿Cuánto costará el arreglo?*
>kwahn-toh kohs-tah-rah ehl ah-rreh-gloh

>I need it as soon as possible.
>*Lo (la) necesito lo más pronto posible.*
>loh (lah) neh-seh-see-toh loh mahs prohn-toh
>poh-see-bleh

>I would like to have this film developed.
>*Quiero que me revele este carrete (rollo).*
>kee-yeh-roh keh meh rreh-beh-leh ehs-teh
>kah-rreh-teh (rroh-yoh)

Other Services

You also might need special services from time to
time. You might, for example, need to find your
consulate to report a lost passport. Or perhaps your
handbag has been stolen and you'd like to file a
police report. You might even want a translator to
make sure you don't get into deeper trouble. The
following phrases should help:

Where is …?
¿Dónde está …?
dohn-deh ehs-tah

> the police station?
> *la comisaría de policía?*
> lah koh-mee-sah-ree-yah deh poh-lee-see-yah

> the American consulate?
> *el consulado americano?*
> ehl kohn-soo-lah-doh ah-meh-ree-kah-noh

> the American embassy?
> *la embajada americana?*
> lah ehm-bah-hah-dah ah-meh-ree-kah-nah

I lost …
Yo perdí …
yoh pehr-dee

my passport.	my wallet.
mi pasaporte.	*mi cartera.*
mee pah-sah-pohr-teh	mee kahr-teh-rah

Help me, please.
Ayúdeme, por favor.
ah-yoo-deh-meh pohr fah-bohr

I need an interpreter.
Necesito un intérprete.
neh-seh-see-toh oon een-tehr-preh-teh

Does anyone here speak English?
¿Hay alguien aquí que hable inglés?
ahy ahl-gee-yehn ah-kee keh ah-bleh een-glehs

14

Is There a Doctor in the House?

In This Chapter

- All about your body
- Signs and symptoms
- Illnesses
- Saying how long you've felt this way

Falling ill when you're away from home is hard enough. The situation becomes even tougher if you can't communicate what's wrong. In this chapter, you learn how to explain your ailments and how long you've been experiencing the symptoms.

Where Does It Hurt?

When traveling, it pays to be prepared if illness strikes. To begin with, familiarize yourself with the parts of the body in Table 14.1.

Table 14.1 Parts of the Body

Body Part	Spanish	Pronunciation
ankle	el tobillo	ehl toh-bee-yoh
arm	el brazo	ehl brah-soh
back	la espalda	lah ehs-pahl-dah
body	el cuerpo	ehl kwehr-poh
brain	el cerebro	ehl seh-reh-broh
calf	la pantorrilla	lah pahn-toh-rree-yah
cheek	la mejilla	lah meh-hee-yah
chest	el pecho	ehl peh-choh
chin	la barbilla	lah bahr-bee-yah
ear	la oreja	lah oh-reh-hah
elbow	el codo	ehl koh-doh
eye	el ojo	ehl oh-hoh
face	la cara	lah kah-rah
finger	el dedo	ehl deh-doh
foot	el pie	ehl pee-yeh
forehead	la frente	lah frehn-teh
gall bladder	la vejiga de la bilis	lah beh-hee-gah deh lah bee-lees
gland	la glándula	lah glahn-doo-lah
hair	el pelo	ehl peh-loh
hand	la mano	lah mah-noh
head	la cabeza	lah kah-beh-sah
heart	el corazón	ehl koh-rah-sohn
hip	la cadera	lah kah-deh-rah
kidney	el riñon	ehl rree-nyohn
knee	la rodilla	lah rroh-dee-yah
leg	la pierna	lah pee-yehr-nah

Body Part	Spanish	Pronunciation
lip	el labio	el lah-bee-yoh
liver	el hígado	ehl ee-gah-doh
lung	el pulmón	ehl pool-mohn
mouth	la boca	lah boh-kah
nail	la uña	lah oo-nyah
neck	el cuello	ehl kweh-yoh
nose	la nariz	lah nah-rees
skin	la piel	lah pee-yehl
shoulder	el hombro	ehl ohm-broh
spine	la espina	lah ehs-pee-nah
stomach	el estómago	ehl ehs-toh-mah-goh
throat	la garganta	lah gar-gahn-tah
toe	el dedo del pie	ehl deh-doh dehl pee-yeh
tongue	la lengua	lah lehn-gwah
tooth	el diente	ehl dee-yehn-teh
wrist	la muñeca	lah moo-nyeh-kah

It Hurts Me Right Here

Do you want to avoid a trip to the doctor while on vacation? The best piece of advice anyone can give you is this: If you don't have a cast-iron stomach, don't drink tap water when you travel. Let's say you ignored this warning, however, because you truly believe Montezuma's Revenge (also known as severe diarrhea) is a thing of the past. You ate salad greens washed in tap water. Or you ordered a drink on the rocks, forgetting the future gastrointestinal effects the ice cubes might have. You've spent the better part of a day in *el baño* (the bathroom), and now you feel you must see a doctor. The obvious first question will be "What's the matter with you?" *"¿Qué le pasa?"* (keh leh pah-sah) To express what hurts or what bothers you, use the expression *tener dolor de (en)* + the part of the body.

> I have a stomach ache.
> *Tengo dolor del estómago.*
> tehn-goh doh-lohr dehl ehs-toh-mah-goh

> He has a pain in his foot.
> *Tiene dolor en el pie.*
> tee-yeh-neh doh-lohr ehn ehl pee-yeh

> I have a toothache.
> *Tengo dolor de muelas.*
> tehn-goh doh-lohr deh mweh-lahs

What Are Your Symptoms?

Suppose your symptoms are more specific than a vague ache or pain. Table 14.2 provides a list of possible symptoms, which will come in handy if you need to describe a problem. Preface your complaint with *"Tengo …"* (tehn-goh, I have …).

Table 14.2 Other Symptoms

Symptom	Spanish	Pronunciation
abscess	un absceso	oon ahb-seh-soh
blister	una ampolla	oo-nah ahm-poh-yah
boil	un divieso	oon dee-bee-yeh-soh

Symptom	Spanish	Pronunciation
broken bone	un hueso roto	oon oo-eh-soh roh-toh
bruise	una contusión	oo-nah kohn-too-see-yohn
bump	una hinchazón	oo-nah een-chah-sohn
burn	una quemadura	oo-nah keh-mah-doo-rah
chills	escalofríos	oon ehs-kah-loh-free-yohs
cough	una tos	oon-ah tohs
cramp	un calambre	oon kah-lahm-breh
cut	un corte	oon kohr-teh
diarrhea	una diarrea	oo-nah dee-yah-rreh-yah
fever	una fiebre	oo-nah fee-yeh-breh
fracture	una fractura	oo-nah frahk-too-rah
indigestion	una indigestión	oo-nah een-dee-hehs-tee-yohn
infection	una infección	oo-nah een-fehk-see-yohn
lump	un bulto	oon bool-toh
migraine	una jaqueca	oo-nah hah-keh-kah
pain	un dolor	oon doh-lohr
rash	una erupción	oo-nah eh-roop-see-yohn
sprain	una torcedura	oo-nah tohr-seh-doo-rah
swelling	una inflamación	oo-nah een-flah-mah-see-yohn
wound	una herida	oon-ah eh-ree-dah

Here are some other phrases that might prove useful when explaining how you're feeling:

I'm coughing.	I'm sneezing.
Toso.	*Estornudo.*
toh-soh	ehs-tohr-noo-doh

I'm nauseous.
Tengo náuseas.
tehn-goh now-seh-yahs

I'm bleeding.
Estoy sangrando.
ehs-toy sahn-grahn-doh

I can't sleep.
No puedo dormir.
noh pweh-doh
dohr-meer

I'm exhausted.
Estoy agotado(a).
ehs-toy ah-goh-tah-
doh(dah)

I hurt everywhere.
Me duele todo el cuerpo.
meh dweh-leh toh-
doh ehl kwehr-poh

I feel bad.
Me siento mal.
meh see-yehn-toh mahl

I'm dizzy.
Estoy mareado(a).
ehs-toy mah-reh-
yah-doh (dah)

I feel weak.
Me siento débil.
meh see-yehn-toh deh-
beel

Telling It Like It Is

The doctor might have to ask you many personal questions about your general overall health and family history. Be prepared—there also will be forms to complete. The doctor or nurse might ask you if you have some of the symptoms or illnesses listed in Table 14.3:

Have you had …?
¿Ha tenido …?
hah teh-nee-doh

Do you suffer from …?
¿Sufre de …?
soo-freh deh

Table 14.3   Other Symptoms and Illnesses

Illness	Spanish	Pronunciation
allergic reaction	una reacción alérgica	oo-nah rreh-ahk-see-yohn ah-lehr-hee-kah
appendicitis	la apendicitis	lah ah-pehn-dee-see-tees
asthma	el asma *(f.)*	ehl ahs-mah
bronchitis	la bronquitis	lah brohn-kee-tees
cancer	el cáncer	ehl kahn-sehr
cold	un resfriado	oon rrehs-free-yah-doh
a chest cold	un catarro del pecho	oon kah-tah-rroh dehl peh-choh
a head cold	el constipado	ehl kohn-stee-pah-doh
diabetes	la diabetes	lah dee-yah-bee-tees
dizziness	el vértigo	ehl behr-tee-goh
exhaustion	la fatiga	lah fah-tee-gah
flu	la gripe	lah gree-peh
hay fever	la fiebre del heno	lah fee-yeh-breh dehl eh-noh
heart attack	un ataque de corazón	oon ah-tah-keh deh koh-rah-sohn
hepatitis	la hepatitis	lah eh-pah-tee-tees
measles	el sarampión	ehl sah-rahm-pee-yohn
mumps	las paperas	lahs pah-peh-rahs
pneumonia	la pulmonía	lah pool-moh-nee-yah
stroke	un ataque de (la) apoplejía	oon ah-tah-keh deh (lah) ah-poh-pleh-hee-yah
sunstroke	una insolación	oo-nah een-soh-lah-see-yohn

Remember to give the doctor any pertinent information that might help him serve you better. You might need some of the following phrases:

> I've had this pain since …
> *Tengo este dolor desde …*
> tehn-goh ehs-teh doh-lohr dehs-deh

> There's a (no) family history of …
> *(No) hay incidencia de … en mi familia.*
> (noh) ahy een-see-dehn-see-yah deh … ehn
> mee fah-meel-yah

> I am (not) allergic to …
> *(No) soy alérgico(a) a …*
> (noh) soy ah-lehr-hee-koh(kah) ah

> I had … years ago.
> *Tuve … hace … años.*
> too-beh … ah-seh … ah-nyohs

> I'm taking …
> *Tomo …*
> toh-moh

> I'm pregnant.
> *Estoy embarazada.*
> ehs-toy ehm-bah-rah-sah-dah

Want to know how serious it is? Ask the following:

Is it serious?	Is it contagious?
¿Es serio (grave)?	*¿Es contagioso?*
ehs seh-ree-yoh	ehs kohn-tah-hee-
(grah-beh)	yoh-soh

How often must I take this medicine?
¿Cuántas veces al día tengo que tomar esta medicina?
kwahn-tahs beh-sehs ahl dee-yah tehn-goh keh
toh-mahr ehs-tah meh-dee-see-nah

How long do I have to stay in bed?
¿Cuánto tiempo tengo que quedarme en cama?
kwahn-toh tee-yehm-poh tehn-goh keh keh-
dahr-meh ehn kah-mah

May I please have a receipt for my medical
insurance?
¿Puede darme una quita para mi seguro médico?
pweh-deh dahr-meh oo-nah kee-tah pah-rah
mee seh-goo-roh meh-dee-koh

Explanations

You might find it necessary to explain how something happened.

I fell.	I cut myself.	I burned myself.
Me caí.	*Me corté.*	*Me quemé.*
meh kah-ee	meh kohr-teh	meh keh-meh

How Long Has This Been Going On?

Your doctor will probably ask how long you've
been experiencing your symptoms. Table 14.4
shows the two ways you might hear the question
posed and shows how to answer each question.

Table 14.4 How Long Have Your Symptoms Lasted?

Question	Answer
¿Cuánto tiempo hace que + present tense of verb …? kwahn-toh tee-yehm-poh ah-seh keh	Hace + time + que + present tense of the verb ah-seh … keh
¿Desde cuándo … + present tense of verb? dehs-deh kwahn-doh	present tense of verb + desde + hace + time
(For) How long have you been suffering? ¿Cuánto tiempo hace que Ud. sufre? kwahn-toh tee-yehm-poh ah-seh keh oo-stehd soo-freh	(I've been suffering) For two days. Hace dos días (que sufro). ah-seh dohs dee-yahs (keh soo-froh)
(For) How long have you been suffering? ¿Desde cuándo sufre Ud.? dehs-deh kwahn-doh soo-freh oo-stehd	(I've been suffering) Since yesterday. (Sufro) Desde hace ayer. (soo-froh) dehs-deh ah-seh ah-yehr

At the Pharmacy

In general, when traveling outside the United States, you should not expect to find a pharmacy that carries the wide range of supplies found in many of our drugstores: stationery, cards, cosmetics, candy, and household items. In the Spanish-speaking world, pharmacies are specifically health-related. They often dispense medicines and drugs over the counter that would require a prescription in the

United States. Many large cities and towns have at least one all-night pharmacy called *una farmacia de guardia* (oo-nah fahr-mah-see-yah deh gwahr-dee-yah). If a drugstore is closed, look on the door for a sign listing the nearest stores that are open.

If you are looking to restock your make-up kit or if you need a bottle of your favorite scent, you must go to *una perfumería* (oo-nah pehr-foo-meh-ree-yah), which specializes in toiletries.

If you are trying to find the closest drugstore, you might want to ask the following:

> Where's the nearest (all-night) pharmacy?
> *¿Dónde está la farmacia (de guardia) más cercana?*
> dohn-deh ehs-tah lah fahr-mah-see-yah (deh gwahr-dee-yah) mahs sehr-kah-nah

When you speak to the druggist, you would say the following:

> I need medication.
> *Necesito medicina.*
> neh-seh-see-toh meh-dee-see-nah

> Could you please fill this prescription (immediately)?
> *¿Podría Ud. ejecutar esta receta (en seguida)?*
> poh-dree-yah oo-stehd eh-heh-koo-tahr ehs-tah rreh-seh-tah (ehn seh-gee-dah)

> How long will it take?
> *¿Cuánto tiempo tardará?*
> kwahn-toh tee-yehm-poh tahr-dah-rah

When you're simply looking for something over the counter, Table 14.5 will help you find it in the *farmacia*, the *perfumería*, or even the *supermercado*. Tell the clerk *"Busco…"* (boos-koh, I'm looking for…) or *"Necesito…"* (neh-seh-see-toh, I need).

Table 14.5 Drugstore Items

Item	Spanish	Pronunciation
For Men and Women		
alcohol	el alcohol	ehl ahl-koh-ohl
antacid	un antiácido	oon ahn-tee-ah-see-doh
antihistamine	un antistamínico	oon ahn-tee-stah-mee-nee-koh
antiseptic	un antiséptico	oon ahn-tee-sehp-tee-koh
aspirin	las aspirinas	lahs ahs-pee-ree-nahs
Band-Aid	una curita	oo-nah koo-ree-tah
brush	un cepillo	oon seh-pee-yoh
comb	un peine	oon peh-ee-neh
condoms	los condones	lohs kohn-doh-nehs
cotton (absorbent)	el algodón hidrófilo	ehl ahl-goh-dohn ee-droh-fee-loh
cough drops	las pastillas para la tos	lahs pahs-tee-yahs pah-rah lah tohs
cough syrup	el jarabe para la tos	ehl hah-rah-beh pah-rah lah tohs
deodorant	el desodorante	ehl deh-soh-doh-rahn-teh

Item	Spanish	Pronunciation
ear drops	las gotas para los oídos	lahs goh-tahs pah-rah lohs oh-ee-dohs
eye drops	las gotas para los ojos	lahs goh-tahs pah-rah lohs oh-hohs
gel	la gomina, la gelatina	lah goh-mee-nah, lah heh-lah-tee-nah
hairspray	la laca	lah lah-kah
heating pad	la almohadilla de califacción	lah ahl-moh-ah-dee-yah deh kah-lee-fahk-see-yohn
ice pack	una bolsa de hielo	oo-nah bohl-sah deh ee-yeh-loh
laxative (mild)	un laxante (ligero)	oon lahk-sahn-teh (lee-heh-roh)
mirror	un espejo	oon ehs-peh-hoh
moisturizer	la crema hidratante	lah kreh-mah ee-drah-tahn-teh
mousse	la espuma	lah ehs-poo-mah
mouthwash	un elixir bucal	oon eh-leek-seer boo-kahl
nail file	una lima	oo-nah lee-mah
nail clippers	el cortauñas	ehl kohr-tah-oo-nyahs
nose drops	las gotas para la nariz	lahs goh-tahs pah-rah lah nah-rees
razor (electric)	la maquinilla de afeitar (eléctica)	lah mah-kee-nee-yah deh ah-feh-ee-tahr (eh-lehk-tee-kah)
razor blade	la hoja de afeitar	lah oh-hah deh ah-feh-ee-tahr
safety pin	el seguro, el imperdible	ehl seh-goo-roh, ehl eem-pehr-dee-bleh

continues

Table 14.5   Drugstore Items   (continued)

Item	Spanish	Pronunciation
scissors	las tijeras	lahs tee-heh-rahs
shampoo (anti-dandruff)	el champú (anti-caspa)	ehl chahm-poo (ahn-tee kahs-pah)
shaving cream	la crema de afeitar	lah kreh-mah deh ah-feh-ee-tahr
sleeping pills	las pastillas para dormir	lahs pahs-tee-yahs pah-rah dohr-meer
soap (bar)	el jabón (una pastilla de jabón)	ehl hah-bohn (oo-nah pahs-tee-yah deh hah-bohn)
suntan lotion	bronceador	brohn-seh-yah-dohr
thermometer	un termómetro	oon tehr-moh-meh-troh
tissues	los pañuelos de papel	lohs pah-nyoo-weh-lohs deh pah-pehl
toothbrush	el cepillo de los dientes	ehl seh-pee-yoh deh lohs dee-yehn-tehs
toothpaste	la pasta dentifrica	lah pahs-tah dehn-tee-free-kah
vitamins	las vitaminas	lahs bee-tah-mee-nahs

For Men Only

after-shave lotion	la loción facial	lah loh-see-yohn fah-see-yahl
cologne	la colonia	lah koh-loh-nee-yah

For Women Only

blush	el colorete de mejillas	ehl koh-loh-reh-teh deh meh-hee-yahs
bobby pins	los pasadores	lohs pah-sah-doh-rehs

Item	Spanish	Pronunciation
cleansing cream	un demaquill-ador	oon deh-mah-kee-yah-dohr
eyeliner	el lápiz de ojos	ehl lah-pees deh oh-hohs
eyebrow pencil	el lápiz de cejas	ehl lah-pees deh seh-hahs
eye shadow	la sombra de ojos	lah sohm-brah deh oh-hohs
foundation	la crema, la base	lah kreh-mah, lah bah-seh
lipstick	el lápiz, la barra de labios	ehl lah-pees, lah bah-rrah deh lah-bee-yohs
make-up	el maquillaje	ehl mah-kee-yah-heh
mascara	el rímel	ehl rree-mehl
nail polish	el esmalte	ehl ehs-mahl-teh
nail polish remover	el quitaesmaltes	ehl kee-tah-ehs-mahl-tehs
powder	los polvos	lohs pohl-bohs
sanitary napkins	las toallas higiénicas	lahs toh-wah-yahs ee-hee-eh-nee-kahs
tampons	los tampones	lohs tahm-poh-nehs
For Babies		
bottle	un biberón	oon bee-beh-rohn
diapers (disposable)	los pañales (desechables)	lohs pah-nyah-lehs (deh-seh-chah-blehs)
pacifier	un chupete	oon choo-peh-teh

Special Items

A pharmacy that specializes in *el alquiler de aparatos médicos* (ehl ahl-kee-lehr deh ah-pah-rah-tohs meh-dee-kohs), the rental of medical appliances, would either sell or have information about the items for the physically challenged featured in Table 14.6.

Where can I get ...?
¿Dónde puedo obtener ...?
dohn-deh pweh-doh ohb-teh-nehr

Table 14.6   Special Needs

Item	Spanish	Pronunciation
cane	un bastón	oon bahs-tohn
crutches	las muletas	lahs moo-leh-tahs
hearing aid	un aparato para sordos	oon ah-pah-rah-toh pah-rah sohr-dohs
walker	un andador	oon ahn-dah-dohr
wheelchair	una silla, un sillón de ruedas	oo-nah see-yah, oon see-yohn deh rroo-weh-dahs

Chapter **15**

Business in Brief

In This Chapter

- How to make a phone call
- Dealing with your mail
- Stationery store supplies
- Faxes and computers

Conducting business in a foreign country is always a bit of a challenge. It's crucial to understand how to place a phone call, send a letter, buy necessary stationery supplies, and deal with faxes. Being computer-literate in any language is probably one of the most important skills you'll need to possess. This chapter helps you deal with all of this.

If you plan to call long distance from a foreign country, whether for business or for pleasure, expect that someone will have to explain how to use the local phone system. It is also likely that the procedures for making local calls will differ from what you are used to back home. You will want to make sure to correctly express the type of call you want to make. Table 15.1 provides you with some options.

Table 15.1   Types of Phone Calls

Type of Call	Spanish	Pronunciation
collect call	una llamada por cobrar, una llamada con cargo	oo-nah yah-mah-dah pohr koh-brahr, oo-nah yah-mah-dah kohn kahr-goh
credit card call	una llamada con tarjeta de crédito	oo-nah yah-mah-dah kohn tahr-heh-tah deh kreh-dee-toh
local call	una llamada local	oo-nah yah-mah-dah loh-kahl
long-distance call	una llamada de larga distancia	oo-nah yah-mah-dah deh lahr-gah dees-tahn-see-yah
out-of-the-country call	una llamada internacional	oo-nah yah-mah-dah een-tehr-nah-see-yohn-nahl

Table 15.2 provides the words to help you understand Spanish directions for placing a phone call.

Table 15.2   How to Make a Phone Call

Action	Spanish	Pronunciation
to call	telefonear, llamar por teléfono	teh-leh-foh-neh-yahr, yah-mahr pohr teh-leh-foh-noh
to call back	volver(ue) a llamar	bohl-behr ah yah-mahr
to dial	marcar	mahr-kahr
to hang up (the receiver)	colgar	kohl-gahr

Action	Spanish	Pronunciation
to insert the card	introducir la tarjeta	een-troh-doo-seer lah tahr-heh-tah
to know the area code	saber la clave de área	sah-behr lah klah-beh deh ah-reh-yah
to leave a message	dejar un mensaje	de-hahr oon mehn-sah-heh
to make a call	hacer una llamada	ah-sehr oo-nah yah-mah-dah
to pick up (the receiver)	descolgar	dehs-kohl-gahr
to telephone	telefonear	teh-leh-foh-neh-yahr
to wait for the dial tone	esperar el tono, la señal	ehs-peh-rahr ehl toh-noh, lah seh-nyahl

Problems

Are you having trouble reaching your party? The following are some phrases you might say or hear when you are having problems:

> What number are you calling?
> *¿Qué número está Ud. llamando?*
> keh noo-meh-roh ehs-tah oo-stehd yah-mahn-doh

> (I have) You have the wrong number.
> *(Yo tengo) Ud. tiene un número equivocado.*
> yoh teh-goh (oo-stehd tee-yeh-neh) oon noo-meh-roh eh-kee-boh-kah-doh

> We got cut off (disconnected).
> *Se nos cortó la línea.*
> seh nohs kohr-toh lah lee-neh-yah

Please redial the number.
Remarque Ud. el número, por favor.
rreh-mahr-keh oo-stehd ehl noo-meh-roh pohr
fah-bohr

The telephone is out of order.
*El teleféno está descompuesto (dañado, fuera de
servicio).*
ehl teh-leh-foh-noh ehs-tah dehs-kohm-pwehs-
toh (dah-nyah-doh, fweh-rah deh sehr-bee-see-
yoh)

There's a lot of static on the line.
Hay muchos parásitos (mucha estática) en la línea.
ahy moo-chohs pah-rah-see-tohs (moo-chah
ehs-tah-tee-kah) ehn lah lee-neh-yah

I'll Write, Instead

It's far more cost-effective to send a letter than to
place a long-distance call. Table 15.3 provides the
vocabulary you need to send your mail.

Table 15.3 Mail and Post Office Terms

Term	Spanish	Pronunciation
address	la dirección	lah dee-rehk-see-yohn
addressee	el destinatario	ehl dehs-tee-nah-tah-ree-yoh
air letter	el correo aéreo	ehl koh-rreh-yoh ah-eh-reh-yoh
envelope	el sobre	ehl soh-breh
letter	la carta	lah kahr-tah

Term	Spanish	Pronunciation
mailbox	el buzón	ehl boo-sohn
package	el paquete	ehl pah-keh-teh
postcard	la tarjeta postal	lah tahr-heh-tah pohs-tahl
postage	el franqueo	ehl frahn-keh-yoh
postal code	el código postal	ehl koh-dee-goh pohs-tahl
postal worker	el cartero (la cartera)	ehl kahr-teh-roh (lah kahr-teh-rah)
rate	la tarifa de franqueo	lah tah-ree-fah deh frahn-keh-yoh
sheet of stamps	la hoja de sellos	lah oh-hah deh seh-yohs
stamp	el sello	ehl seh-yoh

If you just need stamps, save time and pick them up at *estancos* (ehs-tahn-kohs), which are authorized to sell tobacco, stamps, and seals. When you're ready to send a letter or postcard home, look for the red and yellow mailboxes.

Getting Service

You've written your letter, folded it, and sealed it in an envelope. All you need to do is find a post office or a mailbox. If you don't know where one is located, simply ask the following:

Where is the nearest post office (mailbox)?
¿Dónde está el correos (el buzón) más próximo?
dohn-deh ehs-tah ehl koh-reh-yohs (ehl boo-sohn) mahs prohk-see-moh

Different types of letters and packages require special forms, paperwork, and special postage rates. It is important to know how to ask for the type of service you need.

What is the postage rate for ...?
¿Cuál es la tarifa de franqueo de ...?
kwahl ehs lah tah-ree-fah deh frahn-keh-yoh deh

Phrase	Spanish	Pronunciation
an insured letter	una carta asegurada	oo-nah kahr-tah ah-seh-goo-rah-dah
a letter to the United States	una carta a los Estados Unidos	oo-nah kahr-tah ah lohs ehs-tah-dohs oo-nee-dohs
an airmail letter	una carta por correo aéreo	oo-nah kahr-tah pohr koh-rreh-yoh ah-ee-ree-yoh
a registered letter	una carta certificada	oo-nah kahr-tah sehr-tee-fee-kah-dah
a special-delivery letter	una carta urgente	oo-nah kahr-tah oor-hehn-teh

I would like to send this letter (this package) by regular mail (by airmail, special delivery).
Quiero mandar esta carta (este paquete) por correo regular (aéreo, urgente).
kee-yeh-roh mahn-dahr ehs-tah kahr-tah (ehs-teh pah-keh-teh) pohr koh-rreh-yoh rreh-goo-lahr (ah-eh-reh-yoh, oor-hehn-teh)

How much does this letter (package) weigh?
¿Cuánto pesa esta carta (este paquete)?
kwahn-toh peh-sah ehs-tah kahr-tah (ehs-teh
pah-keh-teh)

When will it arrive?
¿Cuándo llegará (llegarán)?
kwahn-doh yeh-gah-rah (yeh-gah-rahn)

I Need Supplies

To successfully conduct any type of business, it is necessary to keep certain basic supplies on hand. No doubt, you'll want to stop at *la papelería* (lah pah-peh-leh-ree-yah), the "stationery store," to stock up on the business items listed in Table 15.4. Start by saying the following:

I would like to buy …
Quisiera comprar …
kee-see-yeh-rah kohm-prahr

Table 15.4   At the Stationery Store

Supply	Spanish	Pronunciation
ballpoint pen	un bolígrafo	oon boh-lee-grah-foh
calculator (solar)	una calculadora (solar)	oo-nah kahl-koo-lah-doh-rah (soh-lahr)
envelopes	unos sobres	oo-nohs soh-brehs
eraser	una goma	oo-nah goh-mah
glue	el pegamento	ehl peh-gah-mehn-toh

continues

Table 15.4 At the Stationery Store (continued)

Supply	Spanish	Pronunciation
notebook	un cuaderno	oon kwah-dehr-noh
paper	papel (m.)	pah-pehl
paper clips	unos sujeta-papeles	oo-nohs soo-heh-tah-pah-peh-lehs
pencils	unos lápices	oo-nohs lah-pee-sehs
pencil sharpener	un sacapuntas	oon sah-kah-poon-tahs
Post-its	unas notas autoadhesivas desprendibles	oo-nahs noh-tahs ow-toh-ahd-eh-see-bahs dehs-prehn-dee-blehs
ruler	una regla	oo-nah rreh-glah
scotch tape	una cinta adhesiva	oo-nah seen-tah ahd-eh-see-bah
stapler	una grapadora	oo-nah grah-pah-doh-rah
stationery	unos objetos de escritorio	oo-nohs ohb-heh-tohs deh ehs-kree-toh-ree-yoh
string	una cuerda	oo-nah kwehr-dah
wrapping paper	papel del envoltorio	pah-pehl dehl ehn-bol-toh-ree-yoh
writing pad	un bloc	oon blohk

Fax It

Let's face it, a fax machine is becoming almost as important as a telephone in many households. When you can transmit and receive messages and

information in a matter of seconds or minutes, you
can speed up the time it takes to transact business.
That translates into extra cash. If you are conducting business in a Spanish-speaking country, it's a
must to be fax-literate.

Do you have a fax machine?
¿Tiene Ud. un fax?
tee-yeh-neh oo-stehd oon fahks

What is your fax number?
¿Cuál es su número de fax?
kwahl ehs soo noo-meh-roh deh fahks

I'd like to send a fax.
Quisiera mandar un fax.
kee-see-yeh-rah mahn-dahr oon fahks

Fax it to me.
Envíemelo por fax.
ehn-bee-yeh-meh-loh pohr fahks

I didn't get your fax.
Yo no recibí (Yo no he recibido) su fax.
yoh noh rreh-see-bee (yoh noh eh rreh-see-
bee-doh) soo fahks

Did you receive my fax?
¿Recibió (¿Ha recibido) Ud. mi fax?
rreh-see-bee-yoh (ah rreh-see-bee-doh) oo-
stehd mee fahks

I'm a Computer Geek

Today a computer is an absolute necessity. The
phrases that follow will help you, even if you're not
a computer geek:

What kind of computer do you have?
¿Qué sistema (tipo, género) de computadora tiene Ud.?
keh sees-teh-mah (tee-poh, heh-neh-roh) deh
kohm-poo-tah-doh-rah tee-yeh-neh oo-stehd

What operating system are you using?
¿Qué sistema operador usa Ud. (está Ud. usando)?
keh sees-teh-mah oh-peh-rah-dohr oo-sah oo-
stehd (ehs-tah oo-stehd oo-sahn-doh)

What word processing program are you using?
¿Qué procesador de textos usa Ud. (está Ud. usando)?
keh proh-seh-sah-dohr deh tehks-tohs oo-sah
oo-stehd (ehs-tah oo-stehd oo-sahn-doh)

What peripherals do you have?
¿Qué periféricos usa Ud. (está Ud. usando)?
keh peh-ree-feh-ree-kohs oo-sah oo-stehd
(ehs-tah oo-stehd oo-sahn-doh)

Are our systems compatible?
¿Son compatibles nuestros sistemas?
sohn kohm-pah-tee-blehs nwehs-trohs
sees-teh-mahs

Something Extra

To say Internet, use the term *el internet*
(ehl een-tehr-neht) or *la Red* (lah rrehd).

To speak about e-mail, you would use the
term *el correo electrónico* (ehl koh-rreh-yoh
eh-lehk-troh-nee-koh).

Useful Idioms and Idiomatic Expressions

An *idiom* is a particular word or expression whose meaning cannot be readily understood by either its grammar or the words used to express it. Idioms defy logic, but they enable you to speak and express yourself in a foreign language the way a native speaker would.

Some idioms are formed with verbs. To use them, simply conjugate the verb to agree with the subject. Make sure that you put the verb in the proper tense (past, present, future) or mood (conditional, subjunctive).

acabar de + inf.	ah-kah-bahr deh	to have just
contar con	kohn-tahr kohn	to rely on
creer que sí (no)	kreh-yehr keh see (noh)	to think so (not)
dar a	dahr ah	to face
dar un paseo	dahr oon pah-seh-yoh	to take a walk
dejar caer	deh-hahr kah-yehr	to drop

esperar que sí (no)	ehs-peh-rahr keh see (noh)	to hope so (not)
hace + time + past	ah-seh	ago
hace buen (mal) tiempo	ah-seh bwehn (mahl) tee-yehm-poh	to be nice (bad) weather
hace calor (frío)	ah-seh kah-lohr (free-yoh)	to be hot (cold)
hace fresco	ah-seh frehs-koh	to be cool
hace sol	ah-seh sohl	to be sunny
hacer viento	ah-sehr bee-yehn-toh	to be windy
hacer una pregunta	ah-sehr oo-nah preh-goon-tah	to ask a question
hacer un viaje	ah-sehr oon bee-yah-heh	to take a trip
hacer una visita	ah-sehr oo-nah bee-zee-tah	to pay a visit
hacerse tarde	ah-sehr-seh tahr-deh	to be getting late
llegar a ser	yeh-gahr ah sehr	to become
prestar atención	prehs-tahr ah-tehn-see-yohn	to pay attention
querer decir	keh-rehr deh-seer	to mean
tardar en	tahr-dahr ehn	to delay in
tener ... años	teh-nehr ... ah-nyohs	to be years ... old
tener calor	teh-nehr kah-lohr	to be warm, hot
tener cuidado	teh-nehr kwee-dah-doh	to be careful
tener dolor de	teh-nehr doh-lohr deh	to have an ache

tener éxito	teh-nehr ehk-see-toh	to be successful
tener frío	teh-nehr free-yoh	to be cold
tener ganas de + infinitive	Teh-nehr gah-nahs deh	to feel like
tener hambre	teh-nehr ahm-breh	to be hungry
tener miedo a + noun	teh-nehr mee-yeh-doh ah	to be afraid of
tener miedo de + inf.	teh-nehr mee-yeh-doh deh	to be afraid to
tener prisa	teh-nehr pree-sah	to be in a hurry
tener que + inf.	teh-nehr keh	to have to
tener razón	teh-nehr rrah-sohn	to be right
tener sed	teh-nehr sehd	to be thirsty
tener sueño	teh-nehr sweh-nyoh	to be sleepy
tratar de + inf.	trah-tahr deh	to try to
volver a + inf.	bohl-behr ah	to (verb) again

Here are some examples showing you how to use these idioms. Note how different subjects, tenses, and moods can be used:

Cuento contigo.	I'm relying on you.
¿Qué quiere decir esto?	What does this mean?
Ellos prestaron atención.	They paid attention.
Es necesario que tengas prisa.	You have to hurry.

Many miscellaneous idiomatic expressions begin with prepositions. They generally refer to time, travel, location, and direction. Many idioms enable you to express your opinions and feelings about things.

a causa de	ah kow-sah deh	because of
a eso de	ah eso deh	at about
a menudo	ah meh-noo-doh	often
a pesar de	ah peh-sahr deh	in spite of
a tiempo	ah tee-yehm-poh	on time
a veces	ah beh-sehs	at times
acerca de	ah sehr-kah deh	concerning
ahora mismo	ah-oh-rah mees-moh	right now
al + inf.	ahl	upon
al fin	ahl feen	finally
algunas veces	ahl-goo-nahs beh-sehs	sometimes
con mucho gusto	kohn moo-choh goos-toh	gladly
cuanto antes	kwahn-toh ahn-tehs	as soon as possible
de acuerdo	deh ah-kwehr-doh	okay
de esta manera	deh ehs-tah mah-neh-rah	in this way
de memoria	deh meh-moh-ree-yah	by heart
de moda	deh moh-dah	in style
de nada	deh nah-dah	you're welcome
de nuevo	deh nweh-boh	again
de pronto	deh prohn-toh	suddenly
de repente	deh rreh-pehn-teh	suddenly
de vez en cuando	deh behs ehn kwahn-doh	from time to time
dentro de poco	dehn-troh deh poh-koh	shortly, soon

en casa	ehn kah-sah	at home
en lugar de	ehn loo-gahr deh	instead of
en medio de	ehn meh-dee-yoh deh	in the middle of
en punto	ehn poon-toh	exactly
en seguida	ehn seh-gee-dah	immediately
en vez de	ehn behs deh	instead of
es decir	ehs deh-seer	that is to say
hasta luego	ahs-tah lweh-goh	see you later
hoy día	oy dee-yah	nowadays
los (las) dos	lohs (lahs) dohs	both
más tarde	mahs tahr-deh	later
muchas veces	moo-chahs beh-sehs	many times
mucho tiempo	moo-choh tee-yehm-poh	a long time
no importa	noh eem-pohr-tah	it doesn't matter
otra vez	oh-trah behs	again
poco a poco	poh-koh ah poh-koh	little by little
por ejemplo	pohr eh-hehm-ploh	for example
por eso	pohr eh-soh	therefore
por favor	pohr fah-bohr	please
por fin	pohr feen	finally
por lo general	pohr loh heh-neh-rahl	in general
por lo menos	pohr loh meh-nohs	at least
por supuesto	pohr soo-pwehs-toh	of course
qué	keh	how, what, what a
sin duda	seen doo-dah	without a doubt
sin embargo	seen ehm-bahr-goh	however
tal vez	tahl behs	perhaps
todavía no	toh-dah-bee-yah noh	not yet
todo el mundo	toh-doh ehl moon-doh	everybody
ya no	yah noh	no longer

Here are some examples using these idioms:

Viajo en avión.	I'm traveling by plane.
No tenemos mucho tiempo.	We don't have a lot of time.
Repita, por favor.	Please repeat.
¿Vas al cine hoy?	Are you going to the movies today?
Tal vez.	Perhaps.

The phrases listed below may be considered mild:

Big deal	*¡No es para tanto!*	noh ehs pah-rah tahn-toh
Cut it out!	*¡Déjate de tonterías!*	deh-hah-teh deh tohn-teh-ree-yahs
I've had it!	*¡Estoy harto de esto!*	ehs-toy ahr-toh deh ehs-toh
It's not worth it.	*¡No vale la pena!*	noh bah-leh lah peh-nah
Leave me alone!	*¡Déjame en paz!*	deh-hah-meh ehn pahs
Mind your own business!	*¡No te metas donde no te llaman!*	noh teh meh-tahs dohn-deh noh teh yah-mahn
No kidding?	*¿De veras?*	deh beh-rahs
No way!	*¡De ninguna manera!*	deh neen-goo-nah mah-neh-rah
You must be kidding!	*¡Qué va!*	keh bah

Spanish–English Dictionary

This dictionary follows international alphabetic order. The Spanish letter combination *ch* and *ll* are not treated as separate letters; therefore, *ch* follows *cg* instead of being at the end of *c*, and *ll* appears after *lk* and not at the end of *l*. Note that *ñ* is treated as a separate letter and follows *n* in alphabetic order.

a   at, to

abrigo (m.)   overcoat

abril   April

abrir   to open

aceite (m.)   oil

aduana (f.)   customs

advertencia   warning

agosto   August

agua (f.)   water

ahora   now

ahorrar   to save

ajo (m.)   garlic

alegre   happy

algodón (m.)   cotton

allá   there

almacén (m.)   department store

alquilar   to rent

alto   tall

amarillo   yellow

anaranjado   orange

anillo (m.)   ring

antes (de)   before

anti-caspa   anti-dandruff

aprender   to learn

aquí   here

arreglar   to adjust, to fix

arroz (m.)   rice

asado baked, roasted

ascensor (m.) elevator

así so, thus

asiento (m.) seat

aterrizar to land

avión (m.) airplane

aviso (m.) warning

ayer yesterday

ayudar to help

azúcar (m.) sugar

azul blue

bajo short

banco (m.) bank

baño (m.) bathroom

bastante enough, quite

basura (f.) garbage

beber to drink

bien well

bienvenido welcome

blanco white

boleto (m.) ticket

bolsa (f.) pocketbook

bonito pretty

botella (f.) bottle

bueno good

buscar to look for

buzón (m.) mailbox

caja fuerte (f.) safe, safety deposit box

cajero automático (m.) automatic teller machine

cama (f.) bed

camarero(a) waiter(ress)

cambiar to change

cambio de dinero (m.) money exchange

camisa (f.) shirt

carne (f.) meat

carta (f.) letter, menu, card

cerca (de) near

césped (m.) lawn

chaleco salvavidas (m.) life vest

champú (m.) shampoo

ciento hundred

cinco (m.) five

cincuenta fifty

cine (m.) movies

cinturón de seguridad (m.) seat belt

claro light, of course

coche (m.) car

collar (m.) necklace

comenzar to begin

comer to eat

comisaría de policía (f.) police station

cómo how

comprar to buy, to purchase

comprender to understand

computadora computer

con with

contestar to answer

contra against

corbata (f.) tie

creer to believe

cruzar to cross

cuál which

cuándo when

cuánto(s) how much (many)

cuarenta forty

cuatro four

cubierto overcast

dar to give

de about, from, of

de nada you're welcome

de nuevo again

debajo de below, beneath, under

deber + infinitive to have to + infinitive

decir to say, to tell

delante de in front of

demasiado too much

desde from, since

después (de) after

detrás de behind

día (m.) day

diciembre December

diez ten

dinero (m.) currency, money

dirección (f.) address

doblar to turn

doce twelve

domingo Sunday

dónde where

dos two

durante during

empleado (m.) employee

en in

en seguida immediately

enero January

enfermo sick

enfrente de in front of

entender to understand

entre among, between

enviar to send

escribir to write

escuchar to listen to

esperar to hope, to wait for, to expect

Estados Unidos (m., pl.) United States

estar to be

este (m.) east

febrero February

firmar to sign

franqueo (m.) postage

frente a   facing, opposite

fuera de servicio   out of order

ganar   to earn, to win

gerente (m.)   manager

gobernanta (f.)   maid service

grande   big

gustar   to like

hablar   to speak, to talk

hacer   to do, to make

hacia   toward

hasta   until

helado (m.)   ice cream

hola   hello

hora (f.)   hour, time

hoy   today

huevo   egg

iglesia (f.)   church

impermeable (m.) raincoat

invierno (m.)   winter

ir   to go

jefe (m.)   department head

joven   young

joya (f.)   jewel

jueves   Thursday

julio   July

junio   June

lápiz (m.)   pencil

largo   long

lavable   washable

lavandería (f.)   laundry/ dry cleaning service

leche (f.)   milk

leer   to read

lejos (de)   far (from)

libro (m.)   book

listo   ready

llave (f.)   key

llegar   to arrive

lugar (m.)   place

lunes   Monday

madre (f.)   mother

maíz (m.)   corn

maleta (f.)   suitcase

malo   bad

mandar   to order, to send

mano (f.)   hand

mantequilla (f.)   butter

manzana (f.)   apple

mañana   tomorrow, morning

marca (f.)   brand name

martes   Tuesday

marzo   March

más   more

mayo   May

medio   half

mejor   better

menos less

mensaje (m.) message

mercado (m.) market

mes (m.) month

mesa (f.) table

metro (m.) subway

mezclar to mix

miércoles Wednesday

mil thousand

mirar to look at, to watch

moneda (f.) coin

montaña (f.) mountain

montar to go up, to ride

mostrador (m.) counter

mucho(s) much (many)

muebles (m. pl.) furniture

museo (m.) museum

muy very

nadie nobody

naranja (f.) orange

negro black

noche (f.) evening, night

norte (m.) north

noticias (f., pl.) news

noventa ninety

noviembre November

novio(a) boy(girl)friend

nueve nine

nuevo new

ochenta eighty

ocho eight

octubre October

oeste (m.) west

oír to hear

ojo (m.) eye

once eleven

ordenador (m.) computer

oro (m.) gold

otoño (m.) autumn

padre (m.) father

pagar to pay

país (m.) country

panadería (f.) bakery

pantalones (m., pl.) pants

papel (m.) paper

para for

parque (m.) park

pasar to pass, to spend time

película (f.) film, movie, roll (film)

pelo (m.) hair

pequeño small

periódico (m.) newspaper

piso (m.) floor (story)

pista (f.) rink, slope, track

poco little, few

pollo (m.) chicken

poner   to put

por   along, by, per, through

por favor   please

por qué   why

precio (m.)   price

preguntar   to ask

prestar   to borrow, to lend

primavera (f.)   spring

primero   first

pronóstico (m.)   weather forecast

pronto   soon

próximo   next

puerta (f.)   door, gate

qué   what

querer   to want

quién   who, whom

quince   fifteen

recibir   to receive

recibo (m.)   receipt

reclamo de bagaje (m.)   baggage claim

reloj (m.)   clock, watch

revista (f.)   magazine

rojo   red

ropa (f.)   clothing

rubio   blond

sábado   Saturday

sacar   to take out

sal (f.)   salt

salida (f.)   departure, exit, gate

salir   to go out, to leave, to deboard, to exit

salsa (f.)   sauce

saludar   greet

sastre (m.)   suit, tailor

seis   six

sello (m.)   stamp

semana (f.)   week

septiembre   September

ser   to be

sesenta   sixty

setenta   seventy

siempre   always

siete   seven

silla (f.)   chair

sin   without

sin duda   without a doubt

sitio (m.)   site, place

sobre   on, upon

subir   to climb, to go up

sucursal (f.)   branch

sur (m.)   south

tabaquería (f.)   tobacco store

también   also, too

tan   as, so

tarde   late

tarde (f.)   afternoon

tarifa   rate

tarjeta (f.)   card

tasa (f.)   rate

temprano   early

tener   to have

tener cuidado   to be careful

tener dolor de   to have an ache

tener éxito   to succeed

tener ganas de   to feel like

tener lugar   to take place

tener prisa   to be in a hurry

tener que + infinitive   to have to + infinitive

tener años   to be years old

tener razón   to be right

tiempo (m.)   time, weather

tienda (f.)   store

tienda de regalos (f.)   gift shop

tienda de ultramarinos (f.)   delicatessen

tirar   to pull, to shoot

todavía   still, yet

todo   all

tomar   to take

traer   to bring

trece   thirteen

treinta   thirty

tren (m.)   train

tres   three

último   last

uno   one

usar   to use, wear

valer   to be worth

veinte   twenty

vender   to sell

venir   to come

venta (f.)   sale

ventana (f.)   window

ventanilla (f.)   window (ticket)

ver   to see

verano (m.)   summer

verde   green

viaje (m.)   trip

viejo   old

viernes   Friday

vivir   to live

volver   to return

vuelo (m.)   flight

ya   already

zapato (m.)   shoe

English–Spanish Dictionary

able (to be able) *poder*

about *de, a eso de*

above *encima de*

to accompany *acompañar*

ad *anuncio* (m.)

address *dirección* (f.)

to adjust *arreglar*

advisable *aconsejable*

after *después (de)*

afternoon *tarde* (f.)

again *de nuevo*

against *contra*

ago *hace + period of time*

to agree with *estar de acuerdo con*

air conditioning *aire acondicionado* (m.)

airline *aerolínea* (f.)

airport *aeropuerto* (m.)

all *todo*

almost *casi*

already *ya*

also *también*

always *siempre*

American consulate *consulado americano* (m.)

American embassy *embajada americana* (f.)

among *entre*

anti-dandruff *anti-caspa*

apple *manzana* (f.)

April *abril*

area code *clave de área* (f.)

arm *brazo* (m.)

around *alrededor (de)*

to arrive *llegar*

ashtray *cenicero* (m.)

to ask *preguntar, pedir*

at *a*

August *agosto*

automatic teller machine *cajero automático* (m.)

bad *malo*

bakery *panadería* (f.)

ballpoint pen *bolígrafo* (m.)

Band-Aid *curita* (f.)

bank *banco* (m.)

bathing suit *traje de baño* (m.)

bathroom *cuarto de baño* (m.), *baño* (m.)

to be *estar, ser*

beach *playa* (f.)

beef *carne de vaca (de res)* (f.)

beer *cerveza* (f.)

before *antes (de)*

to begin *comenzar*

behind *detrás (de)*

bellman *portero* (m.)

below *debajo de*

beneath *debajo de*

better *mejor*

between *entre*

big *grande*

bill *factura* (f.)

black *negro*

blanket *manta* (f.)

blouse *blusa* (f.)

blue *azul*

to board *abordar*

book *libro* (m.)

bookstore *librería* (f.)

booth (phone) *cabina (casilla) telefónica* (f.)

to borrow *prestar*

bottle *botella* (f.)

box *caja* (f.)

branch (office) *sucursal* (f.)

brand name *marca* (f.)

bread *pan* (m.)

to bring *traer*

brother *hermano* (m.)

brown *pardo, marrón*

bullfight *corrida*

bus *autobús* (m.)

butcher shop *carnicería* (f.)

butter *mantequilla* (f.)

button *botón* (m.)

to buy *comprar*

by *por*

calculator *calculadora* solar *solar* (f.)

to call *telefonear, llamar por teléfono*

camera *cámara* (f.)

can *lata* (f.)

candy *dulces* (m., pl.)

candy store *confitería* (f.)

car *coche* (m.), *automóvil* (m.), *carro* (m.)

cash *dinero* (m.)

to cash a check *cobrar un cheque*

cashier *cajero* (m.)

chair *silla* (f.)

to change *cambiar*

change (coins) *moneda* (f.)

check *cheque* (m.)

checkbook *chequera* (f.)

cheese *queso* (m.)

chicken *pollo* (m.)

church *iglesia* (f.)

clock *reloj* (m.)

coffee *café* (m.)

cold, to be cold (person) *tener frío*

cold, to be cold (weather) *hacer frío*

to come *venir*

computer *computadora* (f.), *ordenador* (m.)

cookie *galleta* (f.)

cordless phone *teléfono inalámbrico*

to cost *costar*

country *campo* (m.), *país* (m.)

cup *taza* (f.), *copa* (f.)

customs *aduana* (f.)

dark *oscuro*

daughter *hija* (f.)

day *día* (m.)

decaffeinated *descafeinado*

December *diciembre*

to decide *decidir*

to declare *declarar*

delicatessen *tienda de ultra-marinos* (f.)

to deliver *entregar*

deodorant *desodorante* (m.)

department store *almacén* (m.)

departure *salida* (f.)

to deposit *depositar, ingresar*

to describe *describir*

to desire *desear*

dessert *postre* (m.)

to dial *marcar*

difficult *difícil*

dirty *sucio* (m.)

disagreeable *antipático, desagradable*

discount *descuento* (m.), *rabaja* (f.)

to do *hacer*

doctor *doctor* (m.), *médico* (m.)

door *puerta* (f.)

downtown *centro* (m.)

dozen   *docena* (f.)

dress   *vestido* (m.)

to drink   *beber*

during   *durante*

e-mail   *correo electrónico* (m.)

early   *temprano*

to earn   *ganar*

east   *este* (m.)

easy   *fácil*

to eat   *comer*

egg   *huevo* (m.)

eight   *ocho*

eighteen   *diez y ocho*

eighty   *ochenta*

electricity   *electricidad* (f.)

elevator   *ascensor* (m.)

eleven   *once*

employee   *empleado* (m.)

to end   *terminar, concluir*

to enjoy   *gozar*

enough   *bastante, suficiente*

entrance   *entrada* (f.)

evening   *noche* (f.)

exchange rate   *tasa* (f.) *[tipo* (m.)*] de cambio*

exit   *salida* (f.)

to explain   *explicar*

facing   *frente a*

far (from)   *lejos (de)*

father   *padre* (m.)

February   *febrero*

fifteen   *quince*

fifty   *cincuenta*

to find   *hallar, encontrar*

first   *primero*

fish   *pescado* (m.)

fish store   *pescadería* (f.)

fitness center   *gimnasio* (m.)

five   *cinco* (m.)

to fix   *arreglar*

flight   *vuelo* (m.)

floor (story)   *piso* (m.)

for   *para, por*

forty   *cuarenta*

four   *cuatro*

fourteen   *catorce*

frequently   *frecuentemente*

Friday   *viernes*

from   *de, desde*

front, in front (of)   *delante (de)*

gasoline   *gasolina* (f.)

gate   *salida* (f.), *puerta* (f.)

gift shop   *tienda de regalos* (f.)

to give   *dar*

glass   *vaso* (m.)

glove   *guante* (m.)

to go   *ir*

to go out   *salir*

good   *bueno*

good-bye   *adiós*

good morning   *buenos días*

government employee   *empleado del gobierno* (m.)

gray   *gris*

green   *verde*

grocery store   *abacería* (f.)

hair   *pelo* (m.)

haircut   *corte de pelo* (m.)

ham   *jamón* (m.)

hamburger   *hamburguesa* (f.)

hand   *mano* (f.)

hanger   *percha* (f.)

happy   *alegre*

hat   *sombrero* (m.)

to have   *tener*

to have an ache (in)   *tener dolor (de)*

to have fun   *divertirse *ie*

to have to …   *tener que* + infinitive

head   *cabeza* (f.)

to hear   *oír*

heart   *corazón* (m.)

hello   *hola*

to help   *ayudar*

here   *aquí*

holiday   *fiesta* (f.)

to hope   *esperar*

hot, to be hot (person)   *tener calor*

hot, to be hot (weather)   *hacer calor*

hour   *hora* (f.)

house   *casa* (f.)

how   *cómo*

how much, many   *cuánto(s)*

hundred   *ciento*

hungry (to be hungry)   *tener hambre*

hurry (to be in a hurry)   *tener prisa*

ice cream   *helado* (m.)

ice cubes   *cubitos de hielo* (m., pl.)

immediately   *inmediatamente, en seguida*

in   *en*

instead of   *en lugar de, en vez de*

jacket   *chaqueta* (f.), *saco* (m.)

January   *enero*

jar   *pomo* (m.)

jelly   *mermelada* (f.)

jewelry store   *joyería* (f.)

to jog   *trotar*

juice   *jugo* (m.)

July   *julio*

June   *junio*

to keep   *guardar*

ketchup   *salsa de tomate* (f.)

key   *llave* (f.), *tecla* (f.)

kitchen   *cocina* (f.)

knife   *cuchillo* (m.)

lamb   *carne de cordero* (f.)

lamp   *lámpara* (f.)

to land   *aterrizar*

to last   *durar*

last   *pasado, último*

late   *tarde*

late in arriving   *en retraso*

laundromat   *lavandería* (f.)

to learn   *aprender*

leather   *cuero* (m.)

leather goods store   *marroquinería* (f.)

to leave   *dejar, salir*

lemon   *limón* (m.)

to lend   *prestar*

lens   *lente* (m.)

less   *menos*

letter   *carta* (f.)

light   *claro*

lighter   *encendedor* (m.)

to like   *gustar*

liquor store   *tienda de licores* (f.)

to listen to   *escuchar*

little   *poco*

to live   *vivir*

long   *largo*

to look at   *mirar*

to look for   *buscar*

to lose   *perder*

lucky (to be lucky)   *tener suerte*

machine   *máquina* (f.)

magazine   *revista* (f.)

maid   *criada* (f.)

maid service   *gobernanta* (f.)

mailbox   *buzón* (m.)

to make   *hacer*

makeup   *maquillaje* (m.)

mall   *centro comercial* (m.)

management   *gestión* (f.)

manager   *gerente* (m.)

March   *marzo*

match   *fósforo* (m.)

May   *mayo*

mayonnaise   *mayonesa* (f.)

to mean   *significar*

menu   *carta* (f.), *menú* (m.)

message   *mensaje* (m.)

milk   *leche* (f.)

mineral water   *agua mineral* (m.)

minute   *minuto* (m.)

mirror   *espejo* (m.)

Monday   *lunes*

money   *dinero* (m.)

money exchange   *cambio de dinero* (m.)

month   *mes* (m.)

monument   *monumento* (m.)

more   *más*

morning   *mañana* (f.)

mother   *madre* (f.)

mouthwash   *elixir bucal* (m.)

movie   *película* (f.)

movies   *cine* (m.)

museum   *museo* (m.)

mushroom   *champiñon* (m.)

mustard   *mostaza* (f.)

napkin   *servilleta* (f.)

near   *cerca (de)*

necessary   *necesario*

to need   *necesitar*

new   *nuevo*

news   *noticias* (f., pl.)

newspaper   *periódico* (m.)

newstand   *quiosco de periódicos* (m.)

next   *próximo*

next to   *al lado de*

nice   *simpático, amable*

nine   *nueve*

nineteen   *diez y nueve*

ninety   *noventa*

nobody   *nadie*

north   *norte* (m.)

November   *noviembre*

now   *ahora*

number   *número* (m.)

October   *octubre*

of   *de*

of course   *por supuesto, claro*

office   *oficina* (f.)

often   *a menudo*

okay   *de acuerdo*

old   *viejo*

on   *sobre*

one   *uno*

onion   *cebolla* (f.)

to open   *abrir*

opposite   *frente a*

to order   *mandar*

out of order   *fuera de servicio*

package   *paquete* (m.)

pants   *pantalones* (m., pl.)

paper   *papel* (m.)

parents   *padres* (m., pl.)

park   *parque* (m.)

to participate *participar*

passport *pasaporte* (m.)

to pay *pagar*

pencil *lápiz* (m.)

pepper *pimienta* (f.)

to phone *telefonear*

phone (public) *teléfono público* (m.)

phone card *tarjeta telefónica* (f.)

piece *pedazo* (m.)

pill *pastilla* (f.)

pillow *almohada* (f.)

pink *rosado*

place *lugar* (m.)

plane *avión* (m.)

plate *plato* (m.)

to play games, sports *jugar*

please *por favor*

pocketbook *bolsa* (f.)

police officer *agente de policía* (m.)

police station *comisaría de policía* (f.)

pool *piscina* (f.)

poor *pobre* (f.)

porter *portero* (m.)

postcard *tarjeta postal* (f.)

postage *franqueo* (m.)

postal code *código postal* (m.)

potato *papa* (f.), *patata* (f.)

pound *quinientos gramos, libra* (f.)

pretty *bonito*

price *precio* (m.)

problem *problema* (m.)

to purchase *comprar*

purple *morado*

to put *poner, colocar*

quickly *rápidamente*

to read *leer*

receipt *recibo* (m.)

to receive *recibir*

red *rojo*

relatives *parientes* (m., pl.)

to remember *recordar*

to repair *reparar*

restaurant *restaurante* (m.)

to return *regresar*

room *cuarto* (m.), *habitación* (f.)

safe *caja fuerte* (f.)

sale *venta* (f.)

salesperson *vendedor* (m.)

salt *sal* (f.)

salt shaker *salero* (m.)

sample *muestra* (f.)

sandal *sandalia* (f.)

Saturday *sábado*

sauce *salsa* (f.)

saucer *platillo* (m.)

to say *decir*

scissors *tijeras* (f., pl.)

seafood *mariscos* (m., pl.)

seat *asiento* (m.)

seat belt *cinturón de seguridad* (m.)

to see *ver*

to sell *vender*

to send *mandar, enviar*

September *septiembre*

seven *siete*

seventeen *diez y siete*

seventy *setenta*

shampoo *champú* (m.)

shirt *camisa* (f.)

shoe *zapato* (m.)

short *bajo, corto*

to show *enseñar, mostrar*

show *espectáculo* (m.)

sick *enfermo*

since *desde*

sister *hermana* (f.)

six *seis*

sixteen *diez y seis*

sixty *sesenta*

skirt *falda* (f.)

slice *trozo* (m.)

slowly *lentamente*

small *pequeño*

to smoke *fumar*

sneakers *tenis* (m., pl.)

so *tan*

sock *calcetín* (m.)

soda *gaseosa* (f.), *soda* (f.)

son *hijo* (m.)

soon *pronto*

sour *agrio*

south *sur* (m.)

South America *Sudamérica* (f.), *América del Sur* (f.)

Spain *España*

to speak *hablar*

to spend money *gastar*

to spend time *pasar*

spicy *picante*

spinach *espinaca* (f.)

spot *mancha* (f.)

spring *primavera* (f.)

stadium *estadio* (m.)

stamp *sello* (m.)

still *todavía*

stockings *medias* (f., pl.)

stopover *escala* (f.)

store *tienda* (f.)

subway *metro* (m.)

sugar *azúcar* (m.)

suitcase *maleta* (f.)

summer *verano* (m.)

Sunday *domingo*

sunglasses *gafas de sol* (f., pl.)

suntan lotion *loción de sol* (f.), *loción para broncearse* (f.)

supermarket *supermercado* (m.)

sweater *suéter* (m.)

sweet *dulce*

swimming pool *piscina* (f.)

T-shirt *camiseta* (f.), *playera* (f.)

table *mesa* (f.)

to take *tomar*

to take place *tener lugar*

to talk *hablar*

tall *alto*

tax *impuesto* (m.)

taxi *taxi* (m.)

tea *té* (m.)

teaspoon *cucharita* (f.)

telephone *teléfono* (m.)

to telephone *telefonear*

telephone book *guía telefónica* (f.)

telephone number *número de teléfono* (m.)

television *televisión*

to tell *decir*

ten *diez*

thank you *muchas gracias*

theater *teatro* (m.)

then *después, luego*

there *allá*

thirteen *trece*

thirty *treinta*

thousand *mil*

three *tres*

throat *garganta* (f.)

through *por*

Thursday *jueves*

ticket *boleto* (m.)

time *tiempo* (m.), *hora* (f.)

time (at what time?) *¿a qué hora?*

time (on time) *a tiempo*

tip (gratuity) *propina* (f.)

tissue *pañuelo de papel* (m.)

to *a*

tobacco store *tabaquería* (f.)

today *hoy*

tomato *tomate* (m.)

tomorrow *mañana*

too *también*

too much   *demasiado*

tooth   *diente* (m.)

toothbrush   *cepillo para los dientes* (m.)

toothpaste   *pasta dentifrica* (f.)

towel   *toalla* (f.)

train   *tren* (m.)

to travel   *viajar*

traveler's check   *cheque de viajero* (m.)

trip   *viaje* (m.)

Tuesday   *martes*

turkey   *pavo* (m.)

twelve   *doce*

twenty   *veinte*

two   *dos*

umbrella   *paraguas* (m.)

under   *debajo de*

to understand   *comprender, entender*

United States   *Estados Unidos* (m., pl.)

until   *hasta*

to use   *usar*

vegetable   *legumbre* (f.)

very   *muy*

to visit   *visitar*

to wait for   *esperar*

wallet   *cartera* (f.)

to want   *querer*

weather   *tiempo* (m.)

weather forecast   *pronóstico* (m.)

Wednesday   *miércoles*

week   *semana* (f.)

welcome   *bienvenido*

well   *bien*

west   *oeste* (m.)

what   *qué*

when   *cuándo*

where   *dónde*

which   *cuál*

while   *rato* (m.)

white   *blanco*

who(m)   *quién*

why   *por qué*

winter   *invierno* (m.)

without   *sin*

to work   *funcionar, trabajar*

to write   *escribir*

yellow   *amarillo*

yesterday   *ayer*

young   *joven*

you're welcome   *de nada*

Index

W-X-Y-Z